Sappho has been constructed as many things: proto-feminist, lesbian icon and even – by the Victorians – chaste headmistress of a girls' finishing school. Yet ironically, as Page duBois shows, the historical poet herself remains elusive. We know that Sappho's contemporary Alkaios described her as 'violet, pure, honey-smiling Sappho'; and that the rhetorician and philosopher Maximus of Tyre saw her, perhaps less enthusiastically, as 'small and dark'. We also know that her seventh-/sixth-century BCE island of Lesbos was riven by tyrannical and aristocratic factionalism and that she was probably exiled to Sicily. Much of the rest is speculative. DuBois suggests that the value of Sappho lies elsewhere: in her remarkable verse, and in the poet's reception – one of the richest of any figure from antiquity. Offering nuanced readings of the poems, written in an archaic Aiolic dialect, duBois skilfully draws out their sharp images and rhythmic melody. She further discusses the exciting discovery of a new verse fragment in 2004, and the ways in which Sappho influenced Catullus, Horace and Ovid, as well as later writers and painters.

PAGE DUBOIS is Distinguished Professor of Classics and Comparative Literature at the University of California, San Diego. Her previous books include *Centaurs and Amazons*; *Sappho Is Burning*; *Slaves and Other Objects*; *A Million and One Gods*; and *Slavery: Antiquity and its Legacy* (I.B.Tauris, 2010).

Sappho is addressed to students encountering the archaic Greek poet in literature and gender studies courses and to general readers aware of recent papyrus discoveries that have unexpectedly enlarged her canon. Original translations and discussions of those new poems, which have cast crucial light on Sappho's concerns with ageing and family relations, make Page duBois' study timely and distinctive. Reading her major fragments closely, while bringing evidence from social history to bear on their content, the author locates Sappho within the political, religious, and artistic milieu of seventh-century BCE Lesbos. She traces Sappho's decisive influence upon later Greek and Roman literary and cultural traditions and then applies current interpretive models from reception studies and queer theory to establish her ongoing significance for contemporary audiences. This volume is an essential resource for everyone captivated by Greco-Roman antiquity.

– Marilyn B. Skinner, Professor of Classics Emerita, University of Arizona

Page duBois' pioneering and original approach to Sappho has had a profound impact not only on Sappho studies but on the way we interpret ancient authors and attempt to understand ancient culture in general. While stressing the complicated nature of Sappho's work, especially in its fragmentary form, and her elusiveness as a literary figure, duBois' *Sappho* explores with wonderful clarity how the intense fascination with Sappho over millennia has given rise to an abundant array of literary adaptations, translations, and myth-making. Dubois' book makes Sappho's rich literary history both accessible and utterly enjoyable, bringing to life ancient Lesbos, the reception and transmission of Sappho in ancient Greece and Rome, and the metamorphosis of Sappho through centuries of translation. In her last chapter, duBois considers how recent developments in queer theory may affect our readings of Sappho's work. Finally, duBois' nuanced, brilliant reading of Sappho's most famous poem, the *Hymn to Aphrodite*, illuminates the rich imagery and passion of Sappho, who remains an intense and lasting presence in the Western imagination.

– Ellen Greene, Joseph Paxton Presidential Professor of Classics and Letters, University of Oklahoma

UNDERSTANDING CLASSICS

EDITOR: RICHARD STONEMAN (UNIVERSITY OF EXETER)

When the great Roman poets of the Augustan Age – Ovid, Virgil and Horace – composed their odes, love poetry and lyrical verse, could they have imagined that their works would one day form a cornerstone of Western civilization, or serve as the basis of study for generations of schoolchildren learning Latin? Could Aeschylus or Euripides have envisaged the remarkable popularity of contemporary stagings of their tragedies? The legacy and continuing resonance of Homer's *Iliad* and *Odyssey* – Greek poetical epics written many millennia ago – again testify to the capacity of the classics to cross the divide of thousands of years and speak powerfully and relevantly to audiences quite different from those to which they were originally addressed.

Understanding Classics is a specially commissioned series which aims to introduce the outstanding authors and thinkers of antiquity to a wide audience of appreciative modern readers, whether undergraduate students of classics, literature, philosophy and ancient history or generalists interested in the classical world. Each volume – written by leading figures internationally – will examine the historical significance of the writer or writers in question; their social, political and cultural contexts; their use of language, literature and mythology; extracts from their major works; and their reception in later European literature, art, music and culture. *Understanding Classics* will build a library of readable, authoritative introductions offering fresh and elegant surveys of the greatest literatures, philosophies and poetries of the ancient world.

UNDERSTANDING CLASSICS

Aristophanes and Greek Comedy	JEFFREY S. RUSTEN Cornell University
Augustine	DENNIS E. TROUT Tufts University
Cicero	GESINE MANUWALD University College London
Euripides	ISABELLE TORRANCE University of Notre Dame
Eusebius	AARON P. JOHNSON Lee University, Tennessee
Homer	JONATHAN S. BURGESS University of Toronto
Latin Love Poetry	DENISE MCCOSKEY & ZARA TORLONE Miami University, Ohio
Martial	LINDSAY C. WATSON & PATRICIA WATSON University of Sydney
Ovid	CAROLE E. NEWLANDS University of Wisconsin, Madison
Pindar	RICHARD STONEMAN University of Exeter
Plutarch	MARK BECK University of North Carolina, Chapel Hill
The Poets of Alexandria	SUSAN A. STEPHENS Stanford University
Roman Comedy	DAVID CHRISTENSON University of Arizona
Sappho	PAGE DUBOIS University of California, Berkeley
Seneca	CHRISTOPHER STAR Middlebury College
Sophocles	STEPHEN ESPOSITO Boston University
Tacitus	VICTORIA EMMA PAGÁN University of Florida
Virgil	ALISON KEITH University of Toronto

SAPPHO

Page duBois

UNDERSTANDING CLASSICS SERIES EDITOR:
RICHARD STONEMAN

Published in 2015 by
I.B.Tauris & Co. Ltd
London • New York
www.ibtauris.com

Copyright © 2015 Page duBois

The right of Page duBois to be identified as the author of this work has been asserted by the author in accordance with the Copyright, Designs and Patents Act 1988.

All rights reserved. Except for brief quotations in a review, this book, or any part thereof, may not be reproduced, stored in or introduced into a retrieval system, or transmitted, in any form or by any means, electronic, mechanical, photocopying, recording or otherwise, without the prior written permission of the publisher.

References to websites were correct at the time of writing.

ISBN: 978 1 78453 360 1 (HB)
         978 1 78453 361 8 (PB)
eISBN: 978 0 85773 985 8

A full CIP record for this book is available from the British Library
A full CIP record is available from the Library of Congress

Library of Congress Catalog Card Number: available

Text design, typesetting and eBook versions by Tetragon, London

Printed and bound in Great Britain by T.J. International, Padstow, Cornwall

Contents

Acknowledgements	xi
Introduction	1
I · Understanding Is a Process, and One Poem	5
II · Sappho of Lesbos	33
III · Sappho in Ancient Greece and Rome	81
IV · Trying to Translate Sappho	113
V · Queer Sappho	155
Sources and Suggestions for Further Reading	175
Index	181

To John, for us

Acknowledgements

All translations of Sappho are by John Daley. The author gratefully acknowledges permission from John Daley and Arion Press to use translations of Sappho's poems originally published in *Poetry of Sappho*, introduction by Page duBois, with wood engravings by Anita Cowles Rearden, in Greek with English translation by John Daley with Page duBois; prints by Julie Mehretu (San Francisco, CA: Arion Press, 2011).

My two lips, eyes, thighs, differ from thy two,
But so, as thine from one another doe;
And, oh, no more; the likeness being such,
Why should they not alike in all parts touch?
Hand to strange hand, lippe to lippe none denies;
Why should they brest to brest, or thighs to thighs?

(JOHN DONNE, 'SAPHO TO PHILAENIS')

Introduction

THIS BOOK IS PART OF the series *Understanding Classics*, each volume focused on a particular figure from the classical world of ancient Greece and Rome. Figure is a good word for describing 'Sappho'. She is no longer a person, not yet an author, a somewhat enigmatic name we use to account not just for a small body of astonishingly beautiful poems, written in the Lesbian dialect of ancient Greek, but also for all the other phenomena that surround that name – the legends, the myths, the stories that follow her, the ways in which she was remembered by both ancient and modern people, and by us, the rich complicated process of remembering and alluding to and citing her and her world, for more than 2,000 years, the thrilling accounts of the discovery of her lost work, buried in the sands of Egypt and in European libraries.

The book begins with the assumption that 'understanding' is a process; it is not aimed at some final mastery of the author Sappho, but rather reflects a moment in a long process of engagement with this poet and her poetry. 'Sappho' is less a person, an author in a modern sense, than a nexus of knowledge, connections, attachments and projections. We cannot retrieve a 'real Sappho', and 'understanding' her, or these phenomena, entails taking account of many investments in the poetry and the stories, over millennia. That is, neither the figure Sappho nor her reader is a stable entity; both alter over time and the project of understanding changes through the process of engagement.

Chapter 1, 'Understanding Is a Process, and One Poem', tries to begin answering the question: Who is Sappho? Why should we care? I address the question of 'understanding', trying to make the issues accessible and pleasurable to readers not necessarily familiar with ancient Greek, or literary and cultural theory. And I aim to illustrate the beauties and wonders of Sappho's poems, reading in detail one of the fragments, the first, a poem summoning Aphrodite, goddess of eros, of sexual desire.

Chapter 2, 'Sappho of Lesbos', presents the canonical Sappho, the poet as understood in antiquity. I here discuss the historical context of the figure Sappho, as far as we can know it. I consider the legacy of Homeric verse, Sappho's position as an aristocrat in the tumultuous world of archaic politics on Lesbos and beyond, the conflicts among populist, tyrannical and aristocratic factions in the seventh and sixth centuries before the 'common era', BCE. I also discuss her place alongside her contemporary Lesbian, Alkaios, and other archaic poets. One aspect is the modern focus on Sappho as a single-minded devotee of the goddess Aphrodite, and the need to situate her more fully in the polytheist context of archaic Lesbos.

Chapter 3, 'Sappho in Ancient Greece and Rome', considers the investments in Sappho in antiquity, from the representation of the poet in Herodotos' *Histories*, in comic drama in ancient Athens, to her place in the Hellenistic world and Longinus' praise of her skill, to Sappho as a point of reference for the works of the Roman poets Catullus, Horace and Ovid, including Ovid's *Heroides*, which presents the Lesbian poet as a tragic heterosexual.

In Chapter 4, 'Trying to Translate Sappho', I survey translations of Sappho's poetry, the problems of a fragmentary body of poetic work in an often unfamiliar dialect of ancient Greek, and the ways in which translators over many centuries have attempted to present her to their contemporaries. I define 'translation' not just as putting her words into English, but also as the 'translation', the transportation, the metamorphosis of the figure of Sappho in many contexts, from Renaissance England to twentieth-century feminist and lesbian activism. This chapter discusses centuries of engagement with and appropriation of Sappho by generations of writers, including not only early modern readers and translators and imitators of her work, but also

Victorian poets and lesbians and feminists throughout the twentieth and into the twenty-first centuries. What is the history of the concept 'sapphic'? I talk about poets beyond Europe, the Argentinian Alejandra Pizarnik, for example, a writer profoundly influenced by this ancient Greek singer.

In this chapter I also discuss the process of translating Sappho today and the volume of Sappho's verse I recently published with the poet John Daley. The discovery and publication in 2004 of an almost complete version of fragment 58, previously known in an almost illegible form, has changed the narrative of Sapphic biography and cast new light on Sappho's poetics and erotics. Chapter 4 uses the discovery as a case study for the argument concerning the volatile nature of any 'understanding' of Sappho, since new discoveries are always possible and continue to alter our assessments of her life and work. It goes on to describe the process of translating the most recent discovery of a fuller version of a Sappho poem, concerning her brothers, a find that enriches our sense of Sappho as sister and as polytheist. This chapter emphasises the unstable and tricky business of understanding and translating a poet whose body of work continues to change as new fragments come to light.

In Chapter 5, 'Queer Sappho', I deliberate on how queer theory has evolved into the twenty-first century, and how this may alter our readings of this archaic poet and offer new avenues of coming to understand her work and the traditions of identification with an often imaginary person. Current queer theory engages with questions about how to write the history of homosexuality; as arguments about nature versus culture have ebbed, in discussing the nature of homoeroticism, issues of periodisation have come to the fore. Does it make sense to discuss the history of homosexuality in the same terms as other sorts of history? Furthermore, such work as Heather Love's *Feeling Backward: Loss and the Politics of Queer History* (2007) has altered the terrain of studies of key figures in the history of homosexuality. How does consideration of Sappho affect these new accounts, and vice versa?

At the end of this volume I include suggestions for further reading and a select bibliography. I have also tried to refrain from overly academic language, a trendy vocabulary and received ideas. My hope is to have made the figure Sappho 'understandable', however ephemerally, to contemporary readers.

I

Understanding Is a Process, and One Poem

WE MIGHT THINK OF UNDERSTANDING as a revelation, a sudden 'getting it', a moment at which all is clear and we understand. Such an experience can be like a lightning bolt, an insight that changes everything and completely rearranges our mental furniture. But the kind of understanding I'm interested in here is different. How can we 'understand' a figure, a name, like Sappho, a person, perhaps, who lived more than 2,000 years ago, and around whom has grown an immense network of understandings? Sappho means different things for different people, and she has done so for millennia.

Understanding Sappho is a project, a process, and in fact an unending and discontinuous engagement with what she means. For some, Sappho is significant because she is one of the greatest poets in the history of humankind. For others, she matters because, although she sang, worked, invented her songs in a patriarchal, male-dominated culture, she was a woman. And her fragmentary verses, almost miraculously surviving over millennia, greatly enhance our understanding of what it was to be a woman in the aristocratic world of the seventh and sixth centuries BCE. For others, Sappho matters deeply because her work illuminates the position of the Aegean island of Lesbos, so close to Asia, and remote from the Greek mainland, and therefore turns our gaze on the ancient Greeks away from Athens and towards a wider, eastern landscape. Some readers of Sappho are fascinated by her erotic life. She wrote about her pleasure and delight and longing, usually in relation to objects of desire with female names, and part of her legacy is an attachment to and admiration for erotic boldness. In time, she was rescued from what was an increasingly censured homoeroticism, same-sex love, and turned into the subject of a tragic story of unrequited heterosexual desire, and this story too had a long life, embellished with invented poems, tragic drama and visual materials. In the eyes of ancient readers, Sappho was often remarked upon for the beauties of her poems, her spare and sublime verse; she was imitated and alluded to with admiration and respect. For scholars over many centuries, the poems of Sappho became elusive objects of desire in their own right. Although the scandal of her same-sex themes may have led to the destruction of many of her poems, some survived and the fragments surfaced, randomly and unpredictably. They were preserved in other ancient authors' fragmentary texts, found on scrap papyrus in dumps in Egypt, stumbled upon in the course of the examination of papyri in European libraries. She became a model for new generations, a model of poetic excellence, of erotic precedence, of feminine confidence in a world hostile to expressions like hers. Her legacy continues, as her poetry and all that surrounds or encumbers or illuminates it travels with it.

So how is it possible to 'understand' all this, to come to terms with all that we inherit in the name of Sappho? 'Understanding' of this sort is a process. We cannot hope to 'master' Sappho, to get a grip on her, to wrestle her to the ground and sum up what she means. Just as the understanding of the culture from which she comes has been transformed over many centuries by archaeology and new discoveries, just as we continue to make more finds and to use models to try to construct a vision of what life in her society might have been, so the readers who come to her work have always been enmeshed in their own historical moments, caught within the horizons that allow for and limit their understanding. We are part of a long history of readers attempting to understand classical antiquity and the various individuals who stand out within it. The focus on these particular personalities can indeed obscure our understanding of all that surrounded them, their objects, their slaves, their engagement with events, great and small, of their lives. As I said earlier, 'Sappho' is less a person, an author in a modern sense, than a focus point, a node within a network of knowledge, connections, attachments and projections. We need to abandon any hope of establishing the 'real' Sappho. Even to call her 'she' is perhaps to commit a fault, to try to see her as a person, with all that that entails for a modern reader, and not just a person, but a female person, with all that that too entails for us.

The joy of reading Sappho's poetry, thinking about this long history of engagement between a changing body of work and a changing set of readers, all this is what I would like to share with the reader now. So I offer just one poem, to point to why the verses of this ancient poet have continued to have a seductive, alluring quality (although to describe it in this way might seem to emphasise its maker as a woman). Hers is a powerful, elegant, mesmerisingly assured voice. This is fragment 1:

>Upon your intricately wrought throne, deathless Aphrodite,
>child of Zeus weaving lures, I beg you
>don't break my heart with longing nor with grief,
>>oh queen,
>
>but come here. If once at another time
>you heard my cry from afar,
>and you responded, and came leaving your father's house –
>>golden –
>
>chariot yoked. Beautiful they brought you,
>quick sparrows over the black earth,
>densely whirring wings from heaven
>>through mid-sky.

> All at once they arrived, and you, blessed goddess,
> a smile on your deathless face,
> asked what I was feeling again and why
> > was I calling again,
>
> and what for myself I most want to happen
> in my frenzied heart? 'Whom again do I persuade
> to take you back into her love? Who,
> > Sappho, is doing you wrong?
>
> 'If she runs off, soon she'll be chasing.
> If she refuses to accept gifts, she'll give them.
> If she doesn't love, soon she will love,
> > even unwillingly.'
>
> Come now again, free me from painful
> care. Whatsoever my heart desires to happen,
> make it happen. You yourself
> > fight on my side.

This is the poem listed first in the work of Sappho.

I'm going to look at this poem very closely, as I was taught to do when first learning Greek, when my professor said to me that reading Sappho was difficult. I want to crawl over the surface of the poem we have inherited, like an ant on a papyrus. For readers who might find this sort of thing tedious, I advise moving on to later chapters that set Sappho in her ancient and modern contexts. But I do think that the sort of engagement that follows gives us a sense of connection with a distant, remote mind, another world, that is difficult, but difficult to achieve through any other means. First, I want to show what a deep, close reading of such a canonical and important text can be. This is the only poem of Sappho that I will go into in such depth. And after commenting on it, we'll move on to the material of other chapters, in which I want to contextualise the creation of the poem, as far as we can reconstruct it, and then to discuss the history of the reception of Sappho.

At the end, I'll return to this poem, and direct attention to it again in light of all the network of history and complication and contradictory interpretations that have surrounded it as it has come down to us after 2,500 years.

But first, a reading.

Fragment 1 comes from the work of Dionysios of Halikarnassos, a teacher of rhetoric who lived at the end of the first century BCE. He cites it in a treatise on literary composition and it is one of the very few Sappho poems for which we seem to have the full text. Although he was born in Asia, on the western coast of what is now Turkey, Dionysios studied in Rome and his major work is devoted to Roman history and a justification of the rule of the Romans, which followed upon that by the Greeks themselves. Another bit of it is quoted by Hephaistion, who wrote about the metres of verse in the second century CE. Dionysios uses the poem to illustrate what he calls exuberant and polished composition, and he places Sappho's alongside another example, that of the Greek orator Isokrates. Their works, characterised as flowery, even florid, and smooth, are contrasted with what Dionysios called the 'austere' style, sterner, harsher. Dionysios himself cultivated what was called an 'atticist' style, one that looked back to the great orators of classical Athens, in contrast to 'asianism', the more decorative and ornate style associated with rhetorical schools of western Asia, especially that of Rhodes. We will see later how other students of literature and rhetoric placed Sappho in the canon of inherited Greek writers, how the writer Longinus, for example, cited her work as demonstrating the sublimity he sought in literary works.

In fragment 1, Sappho begins with the word *poikilothron'*, translated here as 'upon your intricately wrought throne'. The word order of Greek differs radically from that of English, in which the normal shape of a sentence or a clause is: subject, then verb, then object: 'I beg you'. Of course, in literary English, this simple skeleton can take a wide range of variations, but the basic order is dominant. In Greek, as in Latin and some other modern languages, it is the form of the word that determines how it functions in a sentence. Just as in English the subject form of the first person is 'I', and the object form is 'me' ('I see you'; 'you see me'), so the form of most Greek words changes according to its grammatical position in a sentence. So 'upon your intricately wrought throne', an adjective defining the goddess Aphrodite, who is addressed in the poem, can come first. And of course, not only can it refer to Aphrodite, but it also opens up the notion that the poem to follow is 'intricately wrought', *poikilon*, exhibiting the variety of colour and shifting light that the Greeks prized. There is some question about the meaning of this word, in fact. *Poikilia* is the quality of variety, of varied colour, of intricacy and ornamentation, as in embroidery or in music. The compound word *poikilo-thron* combines the idea of variety and intricate work with another element, *thron*. Some translators render it as 'throne'; others look to the meaning of *thronon*, 'flowers embroidered on cloth', and see Aphrodite as perhaps garlanded with a richly embroidered variety of flowers. Both meanings, perhaps both present, ambiguously, allow for the beginning of the poem to refer not only to the attributes of the goddess but also to the rich variety of language that will follow.

And what follows establishes the divinity of the addressee of the poem, the goddess Aphrodite, who is here called *athanat'*, that is, 'deathless'. These two first words are adjectives defining the goddess and appear in the case that indicates address, words aimed at an audience, a special situation of language that is marked strongly in ancient Greek. The word *athanat'* is part of a set of words called 'alpha privatives', that is, they contain a root that is negated by a prefatory syllable, just as the English word unusual is made up of 'usual' and the depriving 'un'. The root of *athanat'* is *thanatos*, the Greek word for death, an event, a state as well as a god. Thanatos the god appears on Greek vases, for example, coming to the battlefield to carry off the corpses of warriors like Sarpedon, son of the great god Zeus, Sarpedon who was born of a mortal woman and is therefore subject to death, not immortal as is his father.

Aphrodite too is immortal, deathless. The dominant story of her birth is recounted in Hesiod's *Theogony*, his account of the creation of the universe, the gods and human beings, both male and female. When the second generation of gods was born to Ouranos and his partner Gaia, after she had created Ouranos, he kept his children hidden in Gaia's womb. Gaia plotted with their son Kronos, whom she armed with an iron sickle. When Ouranos came to Gaia in the night, Kronos lay in wait with the sickle and chopped off his father's genitals and threw them behind him. The bloody drops fertilised Gaia and she bore the Furies and the Giants. The genitals were thrown into the sea and from the foam, *aphros*, was born the maiden Aphrodite. Her birth, for Hesiod, bears the signs of her powers, powers of deception as well as love and pleasure. The ambiguity, the double nature of her creation, from violence and castration, to the stormy sea, to the beauty who emerges on grassy Cyprus, is central to Sappho's work, even though Aphrodite is not the only immortal whom Sappho acknowledges. Worship of Aphrodite was associated with Cyprus, and this island, so far east in the Aegean, so close to Asia, may point to the implicit strangeness of the goddess. Some scholars trace her antecedents to ancient Near and Middle Eastern goddesses of fertility such as Inanna, Ishtar and Astarte, and she is sometimes seen as combining the domain of eros with a military aspect that is part of a legacy, perhaps, inherited from these Mesopotamian and Canaanite figures. Sappho's island, Lesbos, lies near the coast of Asia as well and, as we will see later, to understand her better is to come to terms with the ways in which she faces eastwards, rather than towards the more familiar metropolis that was Athens in the classical period.

This paradoxical nature, bloody and destructive, as well as the force that through the green fuse drives the flower, as Dylan Thomas calls it, the energy for sexual union, pleasure and sometimes reproduction, characterises the Greeks' relationship to the goddess Aphrodite. In Plato's *Republic*, the great tragedian Sophocles is said to have blessed his old age, when the torments of Aphrodite, of lust and unreciprocated desire, at last lost their hold on him. A friend asks about his aphrodisiac activities, his devotions to Aphrodite, and he replies that he has run away from them gladly, as from a raving and beastly/savage/wild master. When in the *Homeric Hymn to Aphrodite*, a poem celebrating the goddess, the singer describes her seduction of the son of the house of Troy, father-to-be of Aineias/Aeneas, founder of Rome, the love-making takes place on a bed covered with the skins of bears and lions, killed by the young hunter. He believes the goddess Aphrodite to be a mortal, and after their love-making, when she reveals herself to him as a huge and beautiful immortal, he is terrified that she will make him impotent.

The nature of Aphrodite, rich in pleasure and violence, matters very much to the poetry of Sappho. The poet, as a devotee of the goddess, acknowledges her power, treats her with respect and seeks to enlist her on her side in the world of eros of the Greeks. As we see later, in the love-spells of classical and later Greek magic, love was seen often as a trouble, a scourge, a stimulant to madness, not the gentle and benign rule of a kindly cupid. The Eros of the Greeks, son of Aphrodite, is appropriately armed with bow and arrow; he can cause terrible pain as well as desire and its gratification, suffering that comes from yearning and desire. Sappho's poetry beautifully registers this ambivalence: fear of the goddess and her powers, respect for the pleasures she can bestow. In this poem, as in others, Sappho is begging for the assistance of an ambiguous and remote force, desire embodied in female form.

The first line, then, of this poem names its addressee, its explicit audience, Aphrodite herself, and reminds her (and the listener) of some of the attributes of the goddess. This beginning follows the form of a Greek hymn, a devotional song that summons or invokes a divinity, mentioning her name, recalling features of her lineage, places she was known to frequent, or other remarkable aspects of her being. These are meant to please the divinity, to show respect and honour, to bring attention to what follows, often a prayer, a request for assistance, general or specific. So here the poet goes on to list other features of Aphrodite's being. She calls her 'child of Zeus', referring to a version of the goddess' birth that avoids the bloody origin from the genitals of the castrated Ouranos. As does Homer, she calls up a more benign origin for her Aphrodite, daughter of the great god Zeus and of Dione, her name the feminine form of Zeus', a goddess worshipped at the oracle site of Dodona and possibly represented in the magnificent female forms of the Parthenon pediment in Athens, where one voluptuous female divinity lounges voluptuously in the lap of another. These are perhaps Dione and her daughter Aphrodite.

The word translated as 'weaving lures', *doloploke*, also gestures outward to a complex of meanings. Like the first word of the poem, this is a sort of portmanteau term, characteristic of Greek, which, unlike Latin, can form new words constantly by yoking two other words together. The first part of the word means 'lures', 'tricks'; it begins as a reference to bait for fish, but then comes to mean deception, craft, cunning, even treachery. The goddess is capable both of clever contrivance but also of betrayal, and so the word allows for the double understanding of her nature, as helper and as the cause of pain. The great figure of *dolos*, of cunning, is Odysseus, who is at the heart of the poems of Homer, so important a shadow, a reference, for Sappho and all the poets of the ancient Greeks.

The ethical valence of trickery seems for these Greeks, at least in the period of Homer and even the time of Sappho, to be different from that of our own day, when people may tend to see lying, the vigorous production of untrue stories in interaction with others, or other forms of deception and trickery, to be reprehensible. But the Greeks, especially in these earlier days, valued what they called *metis*, sometimes translated as 'cunning intelligence', and its manifestations in situations where slipping away from trouble is required. Dolon, a Trojan warrior, disguises himself as a wolf in order to penetrate the Greek lines in the siege at Troy. Odysseus is said to have attempted trickery, feigning madness in order to avoid going with the Greeks to Troy in the expedition to retrieve Helen from Paris, son of the ruler of Troy, Priam. *Dolos*, 'cunning', is deployed by the god Hephaistos when he catches his partner Aphrodite in bed with her lover Ares; he weaves a net of gold to trap them and the other gods come both to laugh and to envy the god of war, Ares, who has enjoyed the favours of the goddess. Penelope, Odysseus' patient wife, weaves the shroud of her father-in-law and then picks it apart every night, with *dolos*, to fend off the suitors who threaten to take over Odysseus' household by possessing his queen. Odysseus devises the trick of the 'Trojan' horse, the huge wooden offering containing the Greek warriors, which results in the fall of Troy. Odysseus lies to many of those he encounters on his voyage back home from Troy, after the victory, to Ithaka, where his family awaits. He lies to Athena, herself disguised as a mortal. At the end of the *Odyssey*, having killed her suitors and revealed himself to Penelope, he goes to find his aged father, living like a slave in grief and squalor. And he lies to his father, saying his name is Eperitos, that he saw Odysseus five years before, and his father is devastated further with grief. At last Odysseus says, 'My father, I am here'. Although in later contexts, as in classical Athenian tragedy, Odysseus is presented as a ruthless manipulator, a rhetorician without scruples, in the Homeric poems he is a hero.

As the inheritor of some aspects of the Middle and Near Eastern goddesses Inanna, Ishtar and Astarte, Aphrodite is associated not just with the pleasures and pains of sexuality but also with war. This was so especially in Sparta, where the people of the city worshipped an armed goddess and her union with Ares, one of the many gods of war, was stressed, as it was on the island of Cyprus, where she landed after her bloody birth from the sea, and on the island of Cythera. Cities on the island of Crete offered sacrifices to the couple Ares and Aphrodite. There were oaths sworn to the lovers by young military recruits and these have been connected by some to homosexual bonds, cultivated particularly in Sparta and Thebes, between young warriors. The famous fifteenth-century CE painting by Botticelli of Venus arriving from the sea on a scallop shell, blown by gentle winds, modestly covering her nakedness and about to be enveloped in a beautiful cloak, renders benign this ancient divinity. But many of the Greeks acknowledged their Aphrodite's military powers.

So we have Aphrodite as a figure of *dolos*, and then we have the second element of this 'epithet', this adjective characterising the goddess, which is *ploke*, meaning 'weaving'. As mentioned above, the most renowned weaver of deception is Penelope, wife of Odysseus, who fends off her suitors with deceit until her husband returns in disguise, lying himself about who he is until he can assemble allies with whom to kill those suitors and his faithless slaves. Weaving is an activity of women. In the household, it was their responsibility to spin, to weave and to make the clothing; many images of domestic life in the classical period show wives and their slaves performing these tasks. Helen weaves, discovered in the citadel of Troy by the messenger of the gods Iris, as she creates a red fabric depicting the struggles of the Greeks and the Trojans on the battlefield below. She is the cause of this catastrophic war that brings so much death, and destruction to the city itself. Although the act of weaving is crucial to everyday life, it can have sinister aspects too. The Moirai, the Fates, the spinners of destiny, were weavers as well, in their spinning and cutting of thread especially, determining the lifespan of human beings. The metaphor of weaving extends not only to the making of works of art, to the beginning and ending of lives, but also to the political domain, where the reconciliation of differing positions and classes is represented as the creation of a fabric, the woven strength of a *polis*, a city-state, created through compromise and persuasion.

Aphrodite, weaver of wiles, is now confronted by the voice of the poem, an 'I', who reveals herself/itself now with the word *lissomai*, that is, 'I beseech', 'I beg'. One can beg, or one can address one's prayer to another; in these lines the voice in the poem directs the prayer to a 'you', the Aphrodite addressed in the 'vocative', the case for direct speech. After the respectful and knowledgeable address, the poem becomes not just a hymn of praise but also a request. Often the gesture of begging, of beseeching some benefit in the gift of a powerful person, is accompanied by grasping the knees of the object of the request. When Odysseus goes to the house of Nausithoos in the *Odyssey*, he is advised to grasp the knees not of the king but rather of the queen of the island, Arete, in order to assure his safety and his return to his home on the island of Ithaka. The gesture of supplication, of entreaty, physically establishes a hierarchy between the supplicant and the one who gives, and here the voice of the poet seems to stand before and below the goddess and her richly decorated throne.

The voice first requests not a positive action, but rather that the goddess refrain from hurting. In what becomes a moment of intimacy, this song is revealed to be not a conventional prayer for prosperity for the city, defeat of enemies, but rather another kind of request. The poet refers to Aphrodite's power to hurt, alluded to earlier, her dominion over eros and war. The speaker in the poem asks the goddess neither with distress/longing/desire, nor with grief/sorrow, to tame her. The first word, *asaisi*, is somewhat ambiguous; it can refer to loathing, distress, even nausea. Yet Sappho uses it in another poem in a clearly erotic context, where she describes the heart of woman as devoured by *asa*, in that poem seemingly referring to longing and desire. So the listener, the reader, still does not understand what is being asked of the goddess. And the second word used of the pains to be spared also has no clear erotic reference. The word translated as 'break' here, *damna*, actually refers often to the taming, the breaking of animals; the line could be translated as 'Don't break my spirit'. This verb, though, used for the breaking in of untamed animals, is also used of the subjection of a woman to her husband. The cognate word *damar*, the tamed one, the domesticated one, the broken one, is used in the *Iliad* for 'wife'. The Greeks, according to some, saw children and adolescents as similar to young animals, running wild; they needed to be domesticated, to be broken in and tamed to enter the order of adults. And young girls especially were regarded as needing this domestication. One shrine dedicated to the worship of the goddess Artemis, the Roman Diana, who was associated especially with the wilderness and with wild animals, featured young girls dressed as bear cubs, dancing in honour of the divinity. So the goddess is supplicated, asked not to break, to tame, the speaker with distress or grief. The word can have an erotic connotation; it can suggest seduction, even rape. It has military associations as well: to break is used in the *Odyssey* of lying in wait, ambushing, killing. Aphrodite has the power to harm, to break, to torment human beings with longing and grief, as she plants desire in their breasts and then denies them their object of desire.

The object of breaking, however, is delayed in the Greek, as the poet repeats the form of address to the goddess, this time calling her *potnia*, 'queen/lady/mistress', a title of honour. It bears connotations of domination. Later Aphrodite is called the mistress of the Erotes, the 'loves'. The 'Sapphic' stanza has three lines, similar in metre, and then a fourth shorter line that often serves to emphasise the words in it, to complete a sentence or a unit of meaning, and continuing the sense of the third line. In this case, the word translated as queen, *potnia*, stands at the beginning of that last, fourth line, and expresses again a sense of deference, of respect for the addressee of the poem. The final emphatic word of the stanza, *thumon*, translated here as 'heart', has a complex set of associations in ancient Greek. It means the force of life, that is, spirit, breath, life itself; it can refer to what we think of as mind, to appetite, to will, to courage, to the site of anger and to the heart as the place of emotions of grief or joy. It is related to a verb meaning 'rage' or 'seethe' as a wind or a river, and is extended to persons, who also can storm and rage in fury. So here too we have an ambiguous reference: *thumos* can mean the heart, affected by desire and longing and eros, or the martial spirit of rage and courage, and the poet commands the goddess, emphatically, not to tame that heart, that spirit.

Following the imperative, softened by the deferential address to her ladyship, the next stanza continues the form of a prayer. After naming, characterising and making a request, the prayer can remind the divinity of former episodes of assistance, finding a precedent that is meant to encourage help in the present instance. So the poet sings, 'but come here', clarifying what kind of benefit is being asked for. The voice in the poem requests the presence of the goddess herself. It reminds her of previous moments of descent into the world of mortals, in order to comfort or compel satisfaction of the speaker's desires. The speaker begins a conditional sentence: if X, then Y. The logic, it suggests, is a sort of trap, an ambush. If once upon a time the goddess complied with the request in a prayer, she should do so again, now. Sappho establishes an intimacy with the divinity, if once, another time, she had heard the poet's voice, the sounds she made, even the playing of her lyre. The Greek here, as elsewhere in the poem, contains much alliteration, the repetition of sounds, an emphasis on alphas and sigmas, 'a's and 's's, in the phrase *tas emas audas aioisa*, calling attention subtly to the fact that Sappho's voice comes in the form of song, artful, flowery, smooth. The last word of the stanza's second line is *peloi*, 'from afar'. The goddess is remote, on her highly wrought throne or garlanded with flowers, in a distant country, at one of her shrines such as those in Athens or on the islands. She once upon a time heard Sappho, and the verb used for 'heard' is in what is called the aorist in Greek, a past tense that denotes a single action. 'You heard', and then the poem moves to describe Aphrodite's flight from on high, from Olympus, the sacred mountain in northern Greece where the gods dwell, down to the presence of the singer.

This stanza begins with the command 'come here' and ends with that same verb, 'come', expressed this time in the past, aorist tense, indicating that this arrival occurred once, in a temporally distant time. The poet describes the scene of the goddess' descent vividly. The third line of this stanza begins with the possessive form of the word 'father'; the poem has already addressed the goddess as the child of Zeus. Here the singer speaks 'of the father's house', understood to be a dwelling fit for the gods. 'Leaving', in a participle, a verbal adjective, has feminine gender here, pointing to Aphrodite herself. The penultimate word of this stanza in the Greek is 'golden', and here the poet uses the stanza form and the flexible word order of Greek to let that adjective 'hang', to be suspended, so that it not only defines the 'house' of the god Zeus, but also moves forward into the next stanza, where it could also apply to the 'chariot', the first word in that stanza. The house is golden, the chariot is golden; the goddess leaves one gloriously precious place in a divine vehicle, like nothing human mortals could possess.

The scene of departure and descent is described with great intensity; the first lines of the third stanza portray a golden chariot, yoked, usually with horses; *arma*, the chariot, can be a war chariot, so the ambiguity in relation to Aphrodite's desired assistance, past assistance is maintained. The adjective *kaloi*, 'beautiful', is still consistent with an ambiguous reading of this earlier descent of the goddess, but then suddenly we see not divine horses bearing this golden chariot, but rather 'quick sparrows'. According to other, later sources, sparrows were notorious for lechery; a lecherous man may even have been called a 'sparrow'. Like the rabbits who breed vigorously in current English, ancient sparrows served as a figure for desire and eros. So the companions of Aphrodite, as she descended once upon a time to earth, responding to the need of her devotee, were these birds. About the black earth they come, a black earth that alludes to the use of this phrase in Homeric epic. The black, the dark earth: the adjective is used to refer to wine, to a wave, to water, to dark-skinned men, and extended metaphorically to refer to death, *thanatos*. When Homer in the *Iliad* describes the death of a hero, Protesilaos, he says 'the black earth had closed him under'. The dark earth is the place of mortals, those subject to death, unlike the divine beings of Olympus who live eternally. In fragment 16 Sappho again uses this phrase in a way that recalls the Homeric epics. Aphrodite comes down from her golden place to encounter a mortal, one who will die.

In the fifth book of the *Iliad*, Homer shows a similar scene, of a god being called to the side of a mortal, the hero Diomedes, one of the greatest of the Greek fighters. He is wounded in battle, and calls out to the goddess Athena to come to him:

> Hear me now, Atrytone, daughter of Zeus of the aegis:
> if ever before in kindliness you stood by my father
> through the terror of fighting, be my friend now also, Athene
>
> (5. 115–17, translated by Richmond Lattimore)

Athena comes to Diomedes, standing close beside him, and tells him not to fight with the gods until later in the battle, when Aphrodite enters the fray; he can wound her with his sharp bronze. Sappho's prayer to her goddess, Aphrodite, turns the request from war to love, even as she maintains the allusion to the battlefield, and to the pattern of pursuit and flight that we see over and over again in descriptions of the war for Troy.

The poet Sappho creates a vivid scene of descent by her goddess, Aphrodite, in her lyric stanza, a golden chariot borne by sparrows with 'densely whirring wings'. This phrase echoes a moment in the *Odyssey*. In a scene set on the island of Ithaka, the home towards which Odysseus strives, his son Telemakhos is taking a manly stand against the suitors who are wooing his mother and consuming all the resources of his father's house. Suddenly the great god Zeus sends two eagles down from his mountain and they turn against each other in a dense whir of wings, intent on destruction, as they rip at each other with their talons and then fly away. This bird omen must refer to the strife in the house of Odysseus and to the coming violence when the hero returns and kills the suitors. It is read accurately by one of the witnesses to the scene in the sky, but the greedy suitors of Penelope cannot take in the warning they have been given and they refuse to depart.

The allusions to epic shadow this part of Sappho's poem and such references deepen our understanding. Sappho is a poet of her age, post-Homeric, that is, writing in the period after the date usually assigned to the composition of the poems of 'Homer', the eighth century BCE. The culture into which Sappho was born looked back to the ancient stories of the battle for Troy and the homecomings of its Greek heroes. The poems formed the substance, the background, of cultural literacy in her 'archaic' world. Sappho knows these poems, the formulaic expressions that the oral tradition used in telling these stories; she moves among them with great ingenuity and care, alluding to common expressions but also torquing them from time to time, so that they conform to her poetic intentions. The world of the *Iliad* is one of warriors, of violence and confrontation, of the pursuit and flight of two heroes engaged in the one-on-one combat of the epic battlefield. The *Odyssey* takes place around the Mediterranean, on islands, in confrontation with many alien cultures and human, semi-human and divine characters.

Sappho knows and uses this material for her own ends, in this poem and in others. The black earth and the dense wings of Homer find a new home in her work.

In this crucial third stanza, we hear and feel the descent of the chariot drawn by sparrows, and the poet draws the scene, as we move with her down 'from the heavens of the air', *ouranoithe-ros*, as the word stretches out over two lines, and the phrase 'through the middle', is delayed until the last, shorter line of the stanza. The geography is complicated; the chariot comes down from the vault of the sky, from heaven, from the seat of the gods, through the 'ether', another form of 'sky', perhaps distinguished from *ouranos*, 'heaven', which bears the name of the god Ouranos/Uranus, offspring and partner of the goddess of earth, Ge/Gaia. The chariot thus leaves divine space, beyond the sight of human beings, enters the sky, moving 'through the middle', *dia messo*, crossing the interval between eternal and mortal worlds. This is an almost cinematic image, dynamic and kinetic, as the birds swoop down to the black earth.

Then, suddenly, she, the goddess, is there. The stanza begins with the word *aipsa*, 'suddenly'. Suddenly they arrived, these beautiful swift birds, with a phrase that echoes the *Iliad*. In a scene represented on the shield of Akhilleus/Achilles, forged by the god Hephaistos at Akhilleus' mother's request, a divinely supernatural shield shows human beings and animals making sounds and moving. The phrase is used of the arrival of warriors besieging a city, in an allusion to the setting of the *Iliad*, the fortress and plain of Troy. Combat and death result from the swift appearance of one set of fighters.

The gesture towards this famous scene on the shield may again be calling up memories of battle, of warriors and death in the field, and here in Sappho's poem, instead of the horses, mortal and divine, of the *Iliad*, we have sparrows. The scene is turned in a more benign, perhaps even slightly mocking or comic direction, away from the heroic environment into one of intimacy between mortal and immortal.

Suddenly the goddess is there, and the setting of this incident in the past is overridden by the overwhelming vividness of this appearance of the immortal. The poet's voice addresses her again, directly, calling her *su*, 'you', without the burden of the hymnal formality of the first lines of the poem. Here Aphrodite is *makaira*, 'blessed one', with the connotation that the blessed ones are the immortals, the gods who do not experience death, who are thus happy, in English 'blessed', although this word betrays another sort of religious sense, in which some ultimate, highest divinity confers a blessing, as one English dictionary puts it: 'enjoying the bliss of heaven'. This is a notion foreign to Greek conceptions of the gods. The immortal gods are happy, fortunate, precisely because they are immortal.

The goddess smiled; the words used of her smiling face recall other moments in the Homeric epics and other contemporary poems. In the *Iliad* Aphrodite brings Helen to her lover Paris inside the citadel of Troy, and the poet calls her 'laughter-loving'. A commentator on the *Homeric Hymn to Aphrodite*, a poem close to the epics, this one a poem of praise that describes the birth of the founder of Rome, Aineias/Aeneas, points out that *philommeides*, 'laughter-loving', may in fact mean 'fond of genitals', in reference to the origins of the goddess in her father's castrated member. This is a commonly used 'epithet' of the goddess; if it means laughter-loving, the word suggests the joyous eroticism she brings as her gift to humankind. Here her smile may be less about pleasure than about a benevolent turn towards the mortal being who has summoned her. But, again, the difference between them bears stress. Aphrodite has a smile on her deathless face. The face of the gods can terrorise: Athena carried the face of the Gorgon on her shield to frighten her enemies. And even Aphrodite, when she reveals herself to mortals, can terrify them. In the *Homeric Hymn to Aphrodite*, after she and the son of Priam, Anchises, make love, after she has lied and told him she is a mortal, she lets him sleep and then stands by his bed. Her head reaches up to the roof and she beams forth with an immortal beauty. He is shocked and afraid when he sees her lovely eyes and begs her not to unman him, 'for a man who goes to bed with the deathless goddesses no longer thrives, no longer flourishes'. Proximity and intercourse with these divinities can be dangerous; the mortal Tithonos, taken up by the enamoured goddess of the dawn Eos, becomes her immortal partner but, because she failed to request of Zeus unending youth for her lover, he shrivels away and becomes merely a strengthless voice behind closed doors. As elsewhere, the use of the so-called 'alpha privative', the adjective with a preface that erases its force, leaves both the positive and negative in the reader's or listener's mind. 'Deathless' not only denotes immortality, but also contains death itself. Aphrodite here shows her goodwill, smiling at her supplicant with her deathless, *athanato*, face.

The poet recalls the past episode, when the goddess descended to her and spoke with her. 'She asked what then, again, was I suffering, or feeling, or enduring.' The word *pepontha*, related to the English word 'passion', in the sense of suffering, to 'passive', refers to experience, to having something done to one. The verb occurs here in the perfect tense (that is, 'what has been done to me?') but has a present meaning as well: 'having experienced what, being in what state currently?' It can suggest a negative experience, to have suffered evil at the hands of another, but can also simply refer to feelings of any kind. *Pathos*, another related word, can mean that which happens, or, later, 'emotion'. So the goddess asks of her worshipper: 'what are you feeling, what are you suffering, what is being done to you?'

The adverb *deute*, translated here as 'again', suggests that this is not the first request voiced by the poet, not the first time that Aphrodite has been summoned, invoked to come to the aid of her devotee in distress. This phrase is coupled with another that links this line with the following, the last of the stanza, in which the word 'again' is repeated, along with 'what'. In this second phrase, it has to be translated as 'why'. 'What have I suffered/experienced, again, and again, why do I call?' This repetition occurs in other erotic poems, where love repeatedly assaults the lover, Eros besieges. These serial attacks of love, or *pothos*, 'desire', 'longing', as Sappho calls it in fragment 22, define the erotic world here, where many objects of desire are named and sought after. This way of understanding eros, the experience of love and desire, differs perhaps from our own, at least in official circles, where the ideal is monogamy. The poet Sappho sings of repeated sieges of desire.

She uses the verb *kalemmi*, 'I call/invoke/summon/invite', which can refer to mortal guests or to the invocation of a divinity. The scene shifts suddenly to the present, as the goddess is summoned for us, listeners and readers, into the poet's presence, into our presence, with the last word of this stanza. She puts the words into the goddess' mouth, indirectly at first:

'why am I calling?' And the next stanza, the next lines, follow up this indirect speech. The word for 'what', or 'why', repeats here, twice in the next to the last line of the fourth stanza, then beginning the fifth. 'What do I wish most for myself to happen?' The words following, 'in my frenzied/ maddened/raving *thumos*', stress first of all the ways in which desire, longing, lust destabilise the self; Aphrodite drives the desiring one mad. In the fourth century BCE Plato will write that one of the types of madness, the highest, is that of the lover, a divine variety of madness, ascribed to the gods Aphrodite and Eros. The description occurs in the same dialogue, the *Phaedrus*, in which Socrates speaks of 'the beautiful Sappho', in which Socrates feels, welling up in his breast, a speech about love. Sappho's use of the word *thumos* here echoes its use in the last line of the first stanza, in which Sappho begs the goddess not to tame her spirit, her heart. Here the poet acknowledges that although she does not want her spirit crushed and dominated, she is maddened.

The line pauses between heart/spirit and another question, one that also repeats a word from earlier, the word *deute*, 'again', suggesting that this scene from the past, in a sort of infinite regress, only recapitulates another, earlier scene. The maddened heart of the poet has suffered this same madness before. Repetition, as noted earlier, characterises the assaults of eros; the sixth-century BCE poet Anakreon, who seems to have written his verses on the island of Samos, refers not only to the repetitive attacks of the god of love on him, but also to the theme of same-sex desire associated with the woman of the island of Lesbos:

> Again, tossing a purple ball,
> golden-haired Eros
> calls on me to play with an
>   ornately sandalled girl.
>
> But she, for she is from well-built
> Lesbos, despises me for my hair,
> white; she is gaping
>   at another girl.

Again and again Eros assaults the lover.

And now the speaker changes. If the voice of the poet, Sappho, has been present in the lines that precede this one, now the goddess herself speaks. The continuity of the first-person singular, from Sappho to Aphrodite, is unsettling at first. There are no quotation marks, no way to indicate a shift in the speaker of the 'I', the first person. At first it seems as if the poet were addressing herself, that she herself takes on the voice of Aphrodite, as if the goddess were part of the poet, an internal speaker, not the formidable divinity who once upon a time stood before the maddened lover. In direct speech, the goddess asks, 'Whom again do I persuade?', again suggesting that such scenes are recurrent between the two. The word *peitho*, 'I persuade', is not merely a verb, a word of action, but also a noun, a substantive, and a goddess herself, the divinity called 'Persuasion'. A later commentator says that Sappho calls Peitho 'the daughter of Aphrodite'. Persuasion occurs usually by fair means, through speech, rather than through compulsion or violence.

In this case the goddess asks whom she should persuade 'again', *aps*, and then things become somewhat messy. The Greek text is difficult to manage here and scholars have struggled to read it, to arrive at a fixed and coherent meaning, to understand it. It may say: 'Whom should I persuade again to lead you into her love?' A question hard to understand. The word *agen*, translated as 'to lead', might also mean 'to be broken', or with another letter read as part of the word, 'to be ranked' once more in your love. Since the words were not separated in the manuscript, textual scholars and editors have to decide where to break the lines, and even to establish the metrical pattern. In this Sapphic stanza, for example, the third line, metrically identical to the first two, spills over into the fourth, which could be seen simply as an extension and lengthening of the third line.

If we take *agen* to mean 'to lead', and the object of the infinitive is *s'*, 'you', then it is the poet, or 'Sappho', who will be led back again into the love, the friendship, of another. This formulation places the power to love, to accept her, in the hands of that other. Has Sappho committed some fault that has led to the estrangement between them? Or has she been replaced by another lover, or simply been rejected or abandoned by the lover? The word *philotata*, translated as 'love' here, can carry a wide range of meanings. The adjectival form, *philos*, is notoriously difficult to translate. Whole books have been written about *philia*, 'love', 'friendship', 'belonging', 'affectionate regard', once upon a time opposed in Christian thinking to *agape*, understood as 'brotherly love', or 'charity'. *Philotes* can carry all these connotations, of being in an inner circle of kinship, of friendship, even of alliance between states, but in Homer it often refers to sexual intimacy. In a beautiful scene in the *Iliad*, Hera uses the divine belt of Aphrodite, who unwraps from around her breasts the fabric that depicts *philotes*, 'love-making', and desire, and persuasive allurement that steals thought away from the thoughtful. Hera puts on the garment and it brings the great god Zeus from his purpose of destruction on the battlefield into the arms of Hera.

> And beneath them the earth burst forth fresh budding grass,
> dewy lotus and crocus and hyacinth,
> dense and soft.
>
> (14. 346–9)

The spring, bursting out on the earth, supports the two gods as they make love, drawing down around them a beautiful golden cloud as glistening drops of dew fall upon the earth. This *hieros gamos*, 'holy love-making', has a sacred quality, like rituals of union in the worship of many gods of the ancient Near and Middle East, as well as in Greece itself. The classical period in Athens saw a sacred union between the god Dionysos and a mortal woman, a ritual to guarantee the fertility of the city's fields and vineyards. And after Zeus and Hera's intercourse, which brings new life to the earth and a fertilising dew, the god sleeps with his sister/wife in his arms, *dameis philoteti*, 'conquered/tamed by love-making'. It is perhaps this *philotes*, this sexual union, that is referred to in Sappho's verse, not just friendship, or closeness, affection, familiarity, but erotic love.

The speech of the goddess continues, as she says: 'Who, Sappho, is doing you wrong?' In an extraordinary move, the divinity addresses the poet by name in the last line of this stanza. In fragment 94, to be discussed later, the human speaker in the poem uses the name in this same form at the beginning of a line, emphatically. In Sappho's Lesbian dialect of Greek, the name is *Psappho*. Here the goddess speaks to her intimately and asks, directly, in the present at the heart of this poem, which recollects her past presence. The word translated here as 'doing you wrong', *adikeei*, incorporates another 'alpha privative', an alpha, an 'a', before the root, *dike*, 'justice', but also 'custom', 'way'. Who is injuring, wrong, behaving unjustly, in the wrong way, to Sappho? The question assumes that right is on her side, and the stanza ends with this emphatic statement of partisanship in Aphrodite's voice.

Then comes the promise of fulfilment, of response to the hymn to the prayer. And it comes in the form of three so-called conditional sentences, in the form 'if X, then Y'. These are neatly contained within the sixth stanza, all pronounced still in the words of the goddess herself: 'If she flees, soon she will pursue.' This sentence calls upon an important trope, a frequently deployed figure in Homeric verse; that is, a warrior, frightened, runs from his opponent, as his opponent pursues him. In a terrible and haunting scene in the *Iliad*, the raging hero Akhilleus pursues the fleeing Trojan hero Hektor, who is running from death. The poem compares Akhilleus to a dog that hunts a fawn, and then, in another simile:

> As in a dream one is unable to pursue someone fleeing
> nor can the one evade nor the other chase him down,
> so the one of them could not catch the other on foot, nor the other escape.
>
> (22. 199–201, trans. Lattimore)

In this nightmarish comparison, hunter and hunted, pursuer and pursued, chaser and chased blur together. Death is embodied in the pursuer. In the hunt, the dog will kill the fawn, but on the battlefield, the warriors have been equally matched until one of them falters and becomes the prey. The two are separated, and the violence and power of the pursuer will be used to destroy the pursued.

This paradigm, hunter and hunted, becomes one of the dominant figures in the ancient Greek mentality. It is not only used in the context of war, but forms part of the legal vocabulary of the classical city. In the context of the law courts, the 'pursuer', the *diokon*, is the technical term for the plaintiff, the prosecutor, in a prosecution. The defendant is called the *pheugon*, 'the accused', 'the defendant'. And this language becomes one of the tropes of erotic poetry as well. One partner pursues, the other flees. Some have argued that in the pederastic relationships of the classical Athenians, the decorous attitude of the boy pursued by an older male was to seem, at least, modestly to resist the attentions of his lover. In one of the tiny shreds of fragments attributed to the fifth-century BCE poet Telesilla, she sings of the virgin goddess Artemis fleeing the river-god Alpheus, and escaping his pursuit.

So Sappho's use of these words, pursuit and flight, draws on the context of war but also on the conventions of erotic play. In fragment 1, the goddess uses the conditional sentence form: 'if she flees (now, in the present tense), soon she will pursue (future tense)'. The goddess promises a reversal of the relationship between hunter and hunted, more similar to that of warriors on the battlefield than to that of hunting dog and prey. The lovers seem interchangeable, the game based on the alternation between pursuit and flight. And the erotic play will continue, the goddess asserts, in answer to her worshipper's plea. If she refuses gifts, rather, she will give them. This practice too belongs to the domain of eros. Many of the magnificent vases of the classical world depict a male lover courting, pursuing his male beloved, with the gift of a cock, or a hare, among other treasures. Often the expression, it appears, of a desire to woo, some of the vases have inscribed on them the name of the object of desire, the pursued, as in 'Hermogenes is beautiful'. Gift-giving should bring favours to the lover, an exchange of one valued commodity for another. In a world of rare but precious things, the giving of gifts, even of flowers, marks the erotic relationship, a hierarchy between the given-to and the giver.

In the poem, thanks to the goddess' intervention, this object of desire, this beloved, will be transformed into the subject of desire, into a lover who gives, who courts. In the established rituals of same-sex courtship of the classical period, about which we know most, which involved an older adolescent or a grown man courting a boy, there is a distinct hierarchy of social power between the partners. The older, courting person, the lover, offers gifts and benefits to a younger, perhaps hesitant, 'beloved'. The practice forms part of the political landscape of the classical city, as the older man initiates the younger into the circles of power and prestige of the *polis*. As will be discussed more fully in Chapter 5, such same-sex erotic relationships were also part of the military domain, and the relationship between Akhilleus and Patroklos, at the heart of the *Iliad*, was seen as belonging to this pattern of affective connection between men.

The alternation between lover and beloved is less common in pairs with significant age difference; the older man has social capital, the younger youth and beauty, and the negotiation through gifts and promises of benefit plays out in a situation of marked inequality. Sappho's fragment 1 is different, in that the interchangeability of the two lovers results from the goddess' entry onto the scene. Some scholars, in fact, have argued that this reciprocity, lover become beloved and vice versa, is a sign of the difference between female same-sex love and the male pederasty we know best from the classical period. What has always struck me most forcefully in this poem, however, is the element of coercion. In the last sentence of the stanza, the poet insists on the power of the goddess to force the affection of the pursued, fleeing, gift-refusing object of desire.

The stanza is composed, as noted earlier, of three 'conditional' sentences, in the form 'if X, then Y'. The last clause begins the third line, and ends by slipping over into the fourth, shorter line: 'And if he/she/it does not love, soon he/she/it will love, even not willing.' The very last word, 'willing', is the only place in this poem that marks the poet's desire for a woman, a female person. The adjective and the participle in Greek carry endings that show whether the noun being described is masculine, feminine or neuter, and it is here that we learn that the unwilling person is feminine. Although translation into English requires that gender be ascribed to her earlier in the poem, as in 'her love', such identification of the lover derives from this later line. Up to this point, except for the naming of Sappho herself in line 20, the listener could not know that the object of desire is female. The ambiguity of the military situation in the earlier part of the poem and the ambiguity concerning the gender of the object of desire in this middle section are both resolved with a single letter, the alpha on the ending of the participle, in the very last, emphatic position in the stanza. It is a girl, a woman, who is unwilling and who will be turned by the goddess.

The prospect of reversal, the goddess' coercion of the woman, may recall the scene in the *Iliad* in which Helen, willing or unwilling adulteress, says to Aphrodite, in the guise of a slave, that she will not serve the bed of the Trojan Paris. She has just stood at the wall of Troy, pointing out the various Greek warriors on the battlefield below to Priam, aged ruler of the besieged city. Although Helen recognises the goddess, she refuses to 'serve' Paris' bed. Angrily, Aphrodite rebukes and threatens her, saying that her terrible love for Helen will turn to hate and the mortal woman will die a sad and ugly death. Aphrodite possesses the power to compel, as Helen learns, and although the scene in Sappho's poem may be lighter, more playful, even parodic, a turning from the menace of the epic Aphrodite, nonetheless the goddess' strength of will echoes in the memory of those who know the *Iliad* and its narrative, the audience of both Sappho's poem and the performances of epic.

The last words of the stanza are 'even unwillingly', with, as noted above, a designation of the beloved who will become the lover as female. Some readers interpret the reversal, the interchangeability of roles in this dyad as a sign that Sappho is subverting the hierarchical relationship traditional in pederastic eros, when one partner is often older and dominant, the other reluctantly submissive. And this poem may suggest that indeed relations between female lovers differ from those between boys and men. Nonetheless, the implicit threat, the enlisting of the goddess to the aid of the speaker, leaves little room for a vision of a gentler, less coercive feminine world of eros. The shadow of compulsion and of the martial role of Aphrodite, even her threat against Helen, also accompanies the playful and teasing mood in the words spoken to 'Psappho'. The object of desire has no choice, no will of her own; even unwilling, she will be made to pursue, to give gifts, to love.

The last stanza of fragment 1 moves from the words of the goddess, recollected from a past episode of assistance, back to the voice of the petitioner. Aphrodite has given her promise and her direct speech ends here. The poem resumes, moving in time from the distant past to the present of the hymn, the current request for aid. The word that begins the stanza, *elthe*, 'come', an imperative addressed to the goddess, repeats the verb used in the second stanza. There it is first used as an imperative: 'come'. And it recurs in the last line of that stanza, *elthes*, 'you came'. The last stanza reiterates the demand and recalls the incident from the past that set a precedent for the present. So the poet says 'come to me now again'. And her following words recall the first stanza, in which the voice of the supplicant expressed her pain and suffering, asking to be relieved of the misery Aphrodite can cause mortals. As the poem ends she asks to be 'freed', delivered from difficult care. Here the emphasis is on her mental state, on the worry, trouble, disquietude she might suffer if denied the gifts Aphrodite has promised. The connotations concern anxiety, trouble in mind.

The poem concludes with two more petitions, requests that the goddess bestow on the supplicant what she needs. First she asks that Aphrodite give her everything she desires, that she carry out Sappho's will and accomplish, fulfil her request. The Greek word *telessai*, 'fulfil', 'accomplish', is related to *telos*, 'end', 'goal', and hints at the proper conclusion to both poem and prayer: that the beloved become lover. The verb is repeated, 'to fulfil', and 'fulfil', as a command, an imperative.

The poet repeats the word *thumos*, discussed above, meaning 'heart', 'spirit', 'will', 'life', 'breath', and couples it with a verb that suggests sexual desire, *imerrei*, 'longs for', 'yearns after', 'desires'. The noun that corresponds to this verb, *imeros*, 'longing', 'desire', is sometimes 'personified', or rather deified. That is, the entity desire is thought of as a divine creature, even a god, that creates and watches over desire. In Hesiod's *Theogony*, an account of the creation of the universe, the gods and human beings, Himeros appears dwelling near the Muses, along with the Graces, and later in the poem Hesiod says that 'desire, which loosens the limbs' drips from the eyes of the three Graces, daughters of Zeus. *Himeros* is not always erotic desire. In the *Odyssey*, Odysseus' son Telemakhos, reminded by Menelaos, husband of Helen, of his father still absent, is overtaken with a longing, a *himeros*, to weep for Odysseus. But the verb used in Sappho's poem connotes a longing, a projection into the future; may it also suggest the possibility of further turns of love, the lover again becoming the beloved? Sappho asks that she get everything she wants, everything her heart desires, and this is an open field of desire.

The very last words of the poem continue the poet's prayer in the imperative mode, not a polite request but a confident claiming of Aphrodite's help, based on the goddess' appearance and tender promise that precede. Here Sappho calls directly to 'you', *su*, 'you yourself', *su auta*. The goddess is not to rely on subordinates, on desire or graces, but to assist in her own person, and the words the poet uses here bring us back, beautifully, to the shadow presence of Aphrodite's military prowess, hinted at throughout the poem. Although Sappho may be insisting on love, not war, this aura of power, the warlike potential of Aphrodite, makes itself felt. The word Sappho uses, *summakhos*, startles with its explicit reference to the battlefield, to war, to the warrior that Aphrodite is, even as in this case the field is the ground between two estranged lovers. *Summakhos* means 'fighter with', 'fellow fighter', 'ally in battle'. The prefix *sum* means 'with', as in *symposium*, 'drinking with, drinking together'. And *makhe* means 'battle', 'combat'. In the *Iliad* it is used of armies, sometimes of single combat, the duels that the greatest warriors fought between battle lines. The verb *summakheo* means to be an ally, to battle in alliance.

So when Sappho commands the goddess 'be my ally in battle', my 'fellow fighter', the terrain of eros, we are reminded, appears not as a site of reciprocity and tenderness but a place with the potential for coercion and even violence. Sappho calls upon Aphrodite to be her ally in a struggle.

The conclusion of this poem then reminds us of Aphrodite's nature; as she was created in the violence of her father's creation, so she can cause suffering and pain as well as pleasure and joy. She is warrior goddess as well as guardian of intercourse and reproduction. If in our present we may have forgotten that love is a battlefield, for the Greek audience of this great archaic poet, the domain of Aphrodite can be one of struggle, of domination and coercion, of a hierarchy between pursuer and pursued, between lover and beloved.

I want this poem to stand at the beginning of our attempt to 'understand' Sappho, to recall how in some ways her work is untranslatable, how an effort is required to think our way back, inasmuch as this is even possible, to another, ancient culture. Archaic Greece is not a site of romantic love of the sort familiar to post-medieval Europe, Britain and the Americas. Our understanding of this great poet, limited as it will always be, should take into account the mysteries, the obscurities, the impenetrability of an alien world. If this poem records the poet's voice, a plea to the goddess Aphrodite to turn the beloved into a lover, if it is a 'well-wrought urn', standing alone, how will the chapters that follow, tracking the concentric circles that surround it, the genealogies it inspires, change our understanding of those lines and their maker?

II

Sappho of Lesbos

WHO OR WHAT IS SAPPHO, who wrote the poem I attended to so closely in Chapter 1? What do we know about her life, her experiences? She lived in the remote past, in the seventh and sixth centuries BCE. In this chapter, I talk about the canonical Sappho, the poet as understood in antiquity, touching on her historical context as far as we can know it. I also consider the legacy of Homeric verse, which is the poetic context in which Sappho composed, wrote, sang and performed. I discuss Sappho's position as an aristocrat in the tumultuous world of archaic politics on Lesbos and beyond, caught up in the conflicts among populist, tyrannical and aristocratic factions. And I will locate her as far as possible alongside her contemporary Lesbian, Alkaios, and other archaic poets. One aspect of this chapter is attention to the later focus on Sappho as a devotee of the goddess Aphrodite, as noted in Chapter 1, in which I analysed the poem calling the goddess to her side. I am concerned here with the need to situate Sappho more fully in the polytheist context of archaic Lesbos. Some of her surviving fragments help us see this aspect of her life and poetry more clearly.

One of the problems involved in 'understanding' Sappho is the dearth of reliable information about a figure so distant in the past. Sappho 'flourished', that is, either lived or was born or was known to be living, according to the ancient Greek calendar, during the 42nd Olympiad. That means during the period when conflict stopped, when the various Greek cities sent delegations and athletes to Olympia, on the mainland of Greece, on the peninsula called the Peloponnesos, between the Adriatic and the Aegean seas. The games and ceremonies at Olympia occurred every four years, and were said to have been founded in 776 BCE in honour of Olympian Zeus, the great father of the gods. Allegedly, according to one version of the establishing of the games, the mortal hero Herakles, later immortalised, after having completed his 'labours', arduous tasks assigned him to expiate crimes, founded the games in honour of his father Zeus. The hero Pelops, son of Tantalos, tantalised eternally in the underworld, had been killed by his father and served up to the gods in order to test their ability to distinguish between human and animal flesh. Before they recognised that they were eating Pelops, the goddess Demeter had consumed part of the child's shoulder; the gods brought him back to life and gave him a new shoulder made of ivory. The lover of Poseidon, god of earthquakes and water and lord of horses, Pelops won a chariot race at Olympia by devious means, bringing down an evil fate on the history of his family, which later included Atreus, Agamemnon and Menelaos, the betrayed husband of Helen. But the part of the Greek mainland on which the Olympic games were afterwards held, among them chariot races like that of Pelops, was called the Peloponnesos, the island of Pelops, after this hero. I cite this story because this part of the Greek world and its sacred site, Olympia, although remote from the Aegean island of Lesbos, Sappho's home, nonetheless had great significance for the various tribes that eventually made up a loose community of 'Hellenes'. And they used the Olympiads, these four-year intervals, as the basis of their calendar.

The dates of Sappho's life are somewhat shaky, though, as are many dates for the ancient world, since the sources for them are so difficult to verify. Sometimes we have to rely on corroborating accounts from other neighbouring societies, on a sort of triangulation from several ancient authorities that confirm each other, or on natural occurrences. The problem, however, is that sometimes one ancient source is merely repeating the information contained in another, so that a chain of misinformation can easily be created over hundreds of years. The 42nd Olympiad claim comes from a very much later text, the *Suda*, or *Fortress*, an encyclopedia not put together until the end of the tenth century of the 'common era', CE, that is, 1,600 years after the life of Sappho that it purports to document: so, closer to antiquity than we are and based on other texts even closer than it was, but still a remote and possibly inaccurate source about archaic Greece.

But, if we take this date seriously, Sappho flourished between 612 and 608 BCE. The *Suda* adds further information concerning Sappho, in two entries. Her father's name was either Simon or Eumenos or Eerigyios or Ekrytos or Semos or Kamon or Etarkhos or Skamandronymos. This last name is especially intriguing because it contains reference to a river not on the island of Lesbos, but in Asia, in what was called Asia Minor, the westernmost part of Asia, now mostly in the nation-state of Turkey. Skamander flowed in the region known as the Troad, that is, the region around the ancient city of Troy, the site of the battle for Helen between Trojans and Greeks from the mainland. So the family of Sappho may have had some roots in, or some connections with, Asia, looking eastwards, rather than westwards to such Hellenic sites as Olympia.

Sappho's mother is called Kleis, and the *Suda* states that Sappho herself was 'a Lesbian from Eressos', that is, from a minor city on the island of Lesbos. Other sources note that she spent most of her life in Mytilene, the principal city of the island. The entry in the *Suda* goes on to comment that she lived at the same time as Alkaios, Stesikhoros and Pittakos, the last a politician of Mytilene. These names, if reliably associated with the name of Sappho, help to establish her lifetime in the late seventh and early sixth centuries BCE. The poet Stesikhoros lived, according to the ancient biographers, in the western part of the Greek world, born in what was called Magna Graecia, 'Great Greece' in Latin, that is, in what is now southern Italy. The Greeks had founded colonies all over the Mediterranean in the earlier centuries, and these colonies, city-states that were often still connected with mother cities, *metropoleis*, back in mainland Greece, were an important presence. They were sometimes very wealthy, as in the case of the cities of Sicily, Syracuse, for example, and they purchased and sold goods and traded extensively both with the territories outside the cities themselves and with the motherland.

*

Sappho of Lesbos lived in Mytilene, an ancient city associated with an early diaspora from mainland Greece. She was one of the 'lyric' poets, that is, a poet whose work was composed to be performed with the lyre or other musical accompaniment. Lyric poets composed what is called monody, that is, poetry for a single voice, as well as choral songs, with choir, leader and dance. 'Epic', the name given to the long narratives recounting the events of an earlier, heroic age, was probably performed by a single bard, a singer perhaps composing as he sang. Fragment 1 of Sappho's verses, discussed in the previous chapter, which summons Aphrodite to her side to be her *summakhos*, her 'fellow fighter', turns the heroic, military language of the epic tradition towards love rather than war, taking for granted its audience's familiarity with that epic world. Homer, or 'Homer', is just a name for what seems to have been an oral tradition of story-telling, looking back from a diminished present towards a glorious past of heroes. Although we have only the *Iliad* and the *Odyssey*, the first a poem of part of the battle before Troy, and the second a poem of the hero Odysseus' return from Troy to his home, the island of Ithaka, the Greeks of Sappho's day knew many more stories of that heroic past. The songs recounting the deeds of those heroes, often descendants of the gods, seem to have been presented in verse. Scholars who studied the oral composition of singers in the twentieth century CE, in what was then Yugoslavia, and in other traditions, recognised familiar elements in their stories, elements that resembled what they knew of Homer. There were repetitions, rhythms and references to many different historical periods in the formulaic style of the poems.

The two great poems we do have, the first 'literature' of Europe, may have taken shape somehow, in a manner still unknown, in the second half of the eighth century BCE. Scholars disagree about the question of authorship; was 'Homer' simply the name of the oral tradition, or a poet who composed with the assistance of writing, with a recently developed Greek alphabet? Did someone dictate the oral compositions to scribes who recorded them? Or did a guild of singers memorise the poems and continue to perform them for hundreds of years? Although their definitive form was established later, they far exceed the European location of their first recording in writing, looking to Asia, to Troy, to the Black Sea and to the West, to what is now

Italy; these aspects may reflect the age of colonisation, when the Greeks were moving around the Mediterranean and establishing trade posts and colonies. Some features of the poems look back to the canonical date of the fall of Troy, in the thirteenth century BCE; weapons and armour, for example, at times appear to reflect that period, and archaeology has established the material reality of what were thought to be purely poetic elements of the epics. Archaeologists discovered the site of Troy and dug it up. They found images of Odysseus' boar's-tooth helmet and the boar's teeth themselves that made up such a helmet. Therefore there is a 450-year gap between the time of the events of the *Iliad*, for example, and the establishing of some version of the poem, and another hundred years until the birth of Sappho. That is to say, a distance like that separating us, in the twenty-first century, from the fifteenth century CE, from before the discovery of the 'New World', the Americas.

From what we can see in the texts, the thinkers, the poets, the singers of the seventh and sixth centuries BCE lived in a culture defined in many ways by this epic tradition. Although our view may be distorted by the fact that only the *Iliad* and the *Odyssey* have come down to us, there were many other stories concerning the ancient heroes circulating in the world of Sappho. The heroic exemplars, the heroes descended from the gods, offered paradigms of ethical conduct, of aristocratic, proper behaviour, as well as martial prowess. We do have plot summaries for other narratives in what is called the 'epic cycle' and other poets of the ancient world refer to and rewrite these stories. In the *Odyssey*, for example, Helen's husband Menelaos recalls the hollow horse in which the Greek warriors hid before they crept out in the night and took the city of Troy; but this episode is not narrated in the *Iliad*. Other incidents, including the arrival of the Amazons to assist the Trojans, and the Greek hero Akhilleus falling in love with their queen, Penthesilea, are known from summaries of other poems in the epic cycle and from works of art. Paris/Alexandros, lover of Helen, killed Akhilleus with an arrow in his only vulnerable part, his ankle; there were other narratives of the battle, of the destruction of Troy and its aftermath, with the enslavement of the city's women, and of the various journeys of the Greek heroes back to their homelands.

These stories provided ethical examples, proofs that the aristocrats of the later period were descended from the gods and vivid and thrilling stories. And Sappho knew them, as did her audience. For centuries 'Homer', or these epic narratives, were the matrix of culture for the Greeks, even as each community perhaps knew different versions of the tales and emphasised different aspects of the legacy. When Sappho asks Aphrodite to be her *summakhos*, her 'fellow fighter', her ally, she is using that cultural inheritance, turning the military language to the service of seduction. In another fragment from a papyrus found in Egypt, Sappho describes an incident from the epic world, one not recounted in the two epic poems we have inherited. Fragment 44 tells of the arrival in Troy of Andromakhe, who after the city's fall will become a slave. But Sappho's poem reflects the joy of a wedding:

> Kypros ...
> the herald came ...
> Idaos – swift messenger ...
>   * * *
>
> And of the rest of Asia ... undying fame:
> 'Hektor and his comrades come bringing a quick-eyed beauty
> from sacred Thebe and from free-flowing Plakia –
> delicate Andromakhe – in their ships over the salt
> sea; there are many gold bracelets, and robes,
> purple and fragrant, highly wrought playthings,
> and countless silver drinking cups, and ivory.'
> So he said ...
> Quickly then a beloved father leapt up
> and word spread all through the wide city to his loved ones.
> At once, the sons of Ilos yoked mules beneath
> fine wheeled carriages, and the whole throng climbed on:
> women and maidens with ... ankles ...
> but apart to themselves, the daughters of Priam.
> And young men harnessed the horses beneath chariots ...
>   Greatly

> charioteers
> like gods
> holy
> set out
> for Ilios ...
> A sweet tuned pipe and the kithara were mingled
> with the sound of castanets. Then so clearly the maidens
> sang a holy melody that into the sky sent
> a wondrous sweet echo ...
> And all through the streets ...
> wine kraters and drinking bowls
> ... myrrh, cassia and frankincense did mingle.
> All the older women started to ululate,
> and all the men sounded out a lovely, boisterous song
> calling Paon, the far-shooting, the lyre skilled one
> as they praised Hektor and Andromakhe like gods.

The singer imagines a scene of rejoicing as Hektor and his companions bring his bride to Troy. Her father and seven brothers had been killed in her homeland by Akhilleus; her fate, after enslavement, was to be passed from man to man as a slave. But here the emphasis is on her beauty and grace, and on the prosperous city that receives her, adorned with precious gold and purple, accompanied by silver and ivory. Music fills the air, along with myrrh and frankincense, aromatics that were used in seduction, in ritual and in sacrifice. The men call on Apollo and they all sing in praise of the godlike bride and groom. Although the setting is the citadel of Troy, rather than the hauntingly beautiful scene in the *Iliad* in which Hektor will foresee the enslavement of his wife, Sappho shows us celebration.

Another of her songs also seems to use the Homeric, heroic backdrop to speak of desire and to deploy the traditional, formulaic language of that epic context otherwise. This is fragment 31, which comes from the treatise of someone called Longinus who wrote, probably in the first century CE, on 'sublimity'. He cites this poem to show Sappho's skill at selection and combination:

He appears to me, that man, an equal to the gods
whoever, opposite you,
    sits and leans close
        to give ear as you are sweetly talking.

And your lovely laugh, which completely
flutters the heart inside my breast,
so when I gaze at you, even for a moment, to speak then
    is no longer possible.

Though my tongue falters
and suddenly delicate fire runs wild under my skin,
and my eyes can no longer focus
    and my ears are buzzing,

as sweat drenched and trembling
seizes all of me, I am greener than grass!
I am little short of dying –
    so I seem to myself.

But all this must be endured inasmuch as a poor person ...

Calling someone equal to the gods, as Sappho does here, as in the previous poem, fragment 44, echoes Homer, who often praises human beings by saying they are godlike, resembling the gods, even *isotheos*, 'equal to the gods'.

But in this instance, rather than a term of admiration for a warrior hero, the word refers to the man who sits opposite 'you', the addressee of this poem. Sappho considers this man fortunate as the gods because of his proximity to this woman, with her sweet voice and lovely laughter. Although this scene was once located by scholars at a wedding feast, it could be any occasion at which men and women celebrate together. What occurs next in the poem, what is recalled by the speaker, was once interpreted by a psychoanalytically inclined reader as a sort of anxiety attack brought on by homoerotic desire.

There is homoerotic desire here, but what is most relevant to our discussion is the way in which Sappho's description of her symptoms seems to echo moments in the epic poems as, for example, in the *Odyssey* when Menelaos breaks down, weeping for his brother slaughtered by his own wife's lover; Sappho describes herself, her heart trembling in her breast.

And she goes on, in what might seem to be a poem of praise, to detail her reaction to looking at her beloved, with emphasis not on jealousy, as some have argued, but rather on the effects of gazing at another. When she merely glances at the woman, she can no longer speak. And in a line difficult to interpret, 'corrupt' as they say, possibly full of errors made by a copyist, she may say that her tongue 'broke', *glossa eage*, using a broken verse; with a hiatus, a sort of gap, almost a gulp, that could replicate the awkwardness of her speech. The poem, of course, exquisite in its composition and in its capture of a state of speechlessness, gives the lie to the claim, or leaves this state of paralysis and silence in the past, as the speaker remembers.

A delicate flame has run under her skin. There is no sight in the speaker's eyes, so, paradoxically, the sight she has been describing, of the woman conversing and laughing with the man, is blotted out. Her ears are humming like bees and sweat, possibly cold, pours down over her. If *psukhros*, 'cold', is the correct reading in this line, the contrast between heat and cold represented here, fire and cold, begins a long tradition of such impossibilities, the coexistence of fire and water, too, used by love poets for centuries to attempt to represent the bodily contradictions that overtake the lover in a state of desire. Certainly there is fire, there is sweat, and these elements may recall the sufferings of battle. The singer of the *Iliad* describes the sweat of each warrior fighting around Akhilleus' beloved Patroklos: 'with labour and sweat (*idro*) the knees and the legs and the feet were ceaselessly spattered, and his hands and his eyes.'

A tremor seizes all of her; the verb *agrei*, 'seizes', means to take, to overtake, capture, kill, even, by hunting to pursue and catch. She is prey to this quaking, and the pursuit and flight described in fragment 1 are turned here against the speaker. She is the victim of her own desire. The last half of this stanza has been the subject of much scholarly discussion. What does Sappho mean when she says she is 'greener than grass'? We understand this, one of many somewhat baffling colour words in Greek, to refer to pallor rather than to the literal colour green. She is greenish-yellow, pale green, pale, like shrubs, honey, mountains, trees. Some scholars believe Greek words for colour refer not to the same chromatic elements we understand as 'colour', but rather to the effects of light, dazzling, sparkling, intense. In the *Iliad*, again, on the plain before Troy, the poet refers to 'green fear', *khloros deos*. The warriors, feasting in their tents and in the city, hear Zeus' thunder, and green fear 'seizes' them. When Odysseus in the *Odyssey* describes his travels to the ends of the earth to visit the dead, they suddenly appear:

> But when with vows and prayers I had supplicated the tribes of the dead, I took the sheep and cut their throats over the pit, and the dark blood ran out. Then there gathered from out of Erebos the spirits of those that are dead, brides, and unwedded youths, and toil-worn old men, and tender maidens with hearts still new to sorrow, and many, too, that had been wounded with bronze-tipped spears, men killed in battle, wearing their blood-stained armour. They came thronging in crowds around the pit from every side, with a fearful shout; and green fear seized me.
>
> (11.34–43)

Sappho's speaker is seized by such a fear, perhaps nauseated, ill and pale and afraid, describing an intense physical reaction to the sight of her beloved. Furthermore, she feels herself to be little short of death. The excess, the hyperbole, 'throwing over', as the Greek rhetoricians called it, serve to emphasise her distress, even to create distance between the person experiencing fear and the imminence of death, and the poet, who recalls this extremity, this exaggeration. The contrast between the dangers of the Homeric battlefield, or the encounter with the dead, and this moment of fear and desire calls attention to what is at stake in love. And again, turns the vocabulary of epic towards lyric and towards eros.

Helen 'of Troy' is a central figure in the epic cycle. She appears in the *Iliad* as the somewhat unwilling partner of Paris, having been forced to leave her husband Menelaos by Aphrodite; Menelaos, with his brother Agamemnon and the great warrior Akhilleus, fight on the plain below Troy to win her back. She appears also in the *Odyssey*, as the wife restored to her husband's side. In other versions of the epic narratives, it is reported that Helen did not in fact go to Troy at all, but was in Egypt throughout the period of the Trojan War and that some simulacrum, some copy of Helen took her place among the Trojans. The sixth-century BCE poet Stesikhoros, who lived in the West, that is, in Sicily and what was called Magna Graecia, 'Great Greece', the settlements of the mainland Greeks in Italy, wrote about the Greeks' western territories, describing Herakles' adventures in these lands, for example, and even mentioning the famous silver mines of southern Spain. He was renowned in antiquity for having written verses blaming Helen (of Troy) for having caused the Trojan War. In revenge for the insult, Helen, worshipped as a goddess in Sparta, blinded him. He wrote a palinode, a poem recanting this version of the story of Troy, saying to her: 'the story's not true; you didn't sail in those benched ships to Troy, nor did you come to Troy's towers.' His words, referred to by Plato in his dialogue the *Phaedrus*, became an emblem of changing one's mind. Stesikhoros' recantation earned him the return of his sight.

The other contemporary poet of Sappho, Lesbian Alkaios, also a resident of Mytilene, condemns Helen as well, and as far as we know did not change his story. We have two fragmentary poems in which he expressed his contempt and hatred for the destruction she brought in her wake. In fragment 42, from a papyrus discovered in Egypt, he accuses Helen as he compares her to Thetis, goddess mother of Akhilleus:

> So the story goes, on account of evil deeds,
> pain once came to Priam and his children, from you, Helen,
> bitter pain, and Zeus destroyed with fire
> sacred Ilion.

Alkaios describes then the marriage of Peleus, a mortal, with Thetis, the goddess, as their *philotas*, their love, flourished, and then came the birth of Akhilleus, best of the demigods. 'But they died on account of Helen, the Phrygians and their city'. The destruction of the Phrygians, the Trojans, their city Troy, is laid at the feet of Helen. And Alkaios does not repent. In another, more damning account of this tragedy, on another fragmentary papyrus from Egypt, Alkaios sang:

> ... and fluttered the heart (*thumos*) of Argive Helen in her breast
> and driven mad by the Trojan man
> who tricked his host, over the sea
> she followed him in his ship
>
> leaving behind in her home her child bereft,
> and the well-spread bed of her husband,
> her heart (*thumo*) persuaded her through eros.

The text is quite fragmentary and difficult to decipher here, but the poem concludes with a denunciation of Helen: 'many of his brothers ... the dark earth ... conquered on the plain of the Trojans, for the sake of that one [Helen]; many chariots in the dust; many quick-glancing ones trodden under foot; in the slaughter.' Although the syntax remains difficult to recuperate in the poem, the blame attributed to Helen is its focus. She is responsible for the city's fall, for deaths and destruction and slaughter.

Much of what we know about her contemporary Alkaios casts light on our understanding of Sappho herself, and not least this attitude towards Helen of Sparta, of Mycenae, of Troy. In another of her most significant songs, fragment 16, also retrieved from the sands of Egypt, Sappho alters the view of Helen found in Stesikhoros' first poem and in Alkaios' work.

> Some men say an army of horse cavalry, others, a mass of foot soldiers,
> and still others claim a host of ships to be the most beautiful thing
> upon the black earth. But I say that thing is
>   what ever one loves.
>
> It should be quite easy to make this understood
> by all. For she who so much surpassed
> in beauty all human beings, Helen, left her husband,
>   the best of all men,

abandoned. She went to Troy sailing off,
and neither did her child nor her own parents
give her much pause, but ...
    led astray ...

    with a light heart ...

Myself now, I am reminded of Anaktoria
who has run off ...

I would rather see her lovely footstep
and the radiant sparkle of her gaze,
than all the chariots of the Lydians and the foot soldiers
    in their armor ...

This is one of the most remarkable of Sappho's poems; its rehabilitation of Helen is only one aspect. It begins with a triad, a three-part statement, not unlike the three 'if now, then soon' of the first fragment. Fragment 16 starts with what is sometimes called a 'priamel', the calling up of a choice among different elements. Here the poet sings, 'some say, some say, some say', using the masculine form for 'some', that is, some men say, and some others say, and some others say. She sets up these various choices only to state her own preference. And, as in the first poem, the battlefield, the situation of war and warriors, shadows the verses.

    The choice is among an army of horsemen, or of foot soldiers, or of ships; each of these bodies is devoted to the waging of war. And upon the black earth, she says, using again that phrase that appeared in the first fragment, and that calls up the vocabulary and the situation of the battlefield of the *Iliad*, the warriors fighting on the dark earth, and buried in it. Some find these armies to be the most beautiful thing on that black earth. Here Sappho provides a sort of philosophy before philosophy, an attempt to provide a definition of something abstract that goes beyond individual choices and preferences. This effort precedes Plato's attempt, two centuries later, to define 'the good', *to kalon*. Sappho wants to see beyond, behind, above the common admiration for a field of horsemen, of infantry, of ships, to what unites them, and what allows for other preferences, other choices. And her preference, it turns out, is a sort of refusal of the military array of male warriors, cavalry, sailors. She offers, though, a general description, an abstract definition of what is 'the most beautiful thing on the black earth', saying it is 'whatever one loves'.

The priamel sets up a wide range of objects of preference, in a move that characteristically, in Greek poetry and prose, suggests an exhaustive catalogue, as in 'land and sea', 'above and below'. She opens up the definition and the possibilities, and uses the priamel as a foil, as a background to her assertion conceived in a more abstract fashion. They say this; I, on the other hand, say that. And that is not, for now, just another of the same sort of army, *stroton*, but an all-encompassing definition that allows for 'their' preferences, but also for hers, and for others as well. And after offering this definition of the most beautiful, she moves on to her proof.

As she says, her claim is easy to support. She can make it 'understandable', to all. The proof concerns Helen. And she suggests that Helen is the perfect example for illustrating her general principle, since she herself surpassed all others in precisely that attribute in question, 'beauty', *kallos*, a word which echoes her previous stanza and her claim about 'the most beautiful thing', *kalliston*. Helen, the most beautiful of human beings, chose as the most beautiful thing not her noble husband, but left him behind, along with her child and her dear parents. Just as she excelled all others in beauty, her husband was 'best of all', *panaristos*, a descendant of that Pelops who won the race at Olympia. But she left him. The word used for leaving, a participle, *kallipois'*, 'abandoning/forsaking/leaving behind', although not related, etymologically, to the same root, as *kallos, kalliston*, 'beauty', 'beautiful', contains the same syllable, *kall*, which binds this participle, 'leaving behind', to the theme of the beautiful. And Helen's quality as the most beautiful of all mortals, therefore most exemplary, qualifies her, and it is as if her beauty itself leads her to leave her family behind and to choose Paris, her Trojan lover.

She went, off, sailing, to Troy, without a thought for husband, child, parents. Leda, the mother of Helen, her sister and their brothers, the twins Kastor and Polydeukes/Pollux, gave birth to two eggs after having been raped, ravished, overpowered by Zeus, who came to her in the form of a swan. The moment is recalled in the great poem of the twentieth-century poet William Butler Yeats, 'Leda and the Swan', published in 1928. 'How can those terrified vague fingers push/ The feathered glory from her loosening thighs?' Yeats reminds the reader of the damage done by this rape, 'the broken wall, the burning roof and town/ And Agamemnon dead'. The figure of Helen haunts the work of this Irish poet. As the most beautiful of all mortals, Helen becomes an emblem of beauty itself.

In the fragment we have of Sappho's sixteenth poem, what follows is an especially broken and difficult piece of the papyrus. Something – Aphrodite, eros, love – turned Helen away, misled her, altered her course, and we cannot yet understand what caused this turn. Nonetheless, the voice in the poem seems not to judge Helen harshly, not to blame her, as did the first Stesikhoros poem, as did Alkaios, for the death of warriors and the destruction of Troy. Homer represents Helen as the child of Zeus. In the myths told of her, in which she is sometimes seen as a goddess herself, it was Aphrodite who gave her as a prize to Paris. He had been chosen as the judge in a contest among the goddesses Aphrodite herself, Hera and Athena. Strife, Eris, had been excluded from the gods' and mortals' celebration of the marriage between the mortal Peleus and the goddess Thetis, mother of Akhilleus. Eris threw a golden apple on which was inscribed 'to the most beautiful', *kalliste*, among the wedding guests; Paris, the judge, was offered power by Hera, wisdom by Athena, the most beautiful woman in the world by Aphrodite. He chose Aphrodite, and she gave him Helen as his reward, even though she had already been married to Menelaos, brother of Agamemnon. The question of Helen's responsibility, her blame for the war that followed her departure from the house of Menelaos, rests on the question of Aphrodite's role. Was Helen the unfaithful adulteress who abandoned her husband and family for lust, or was she the instrument, the guiltless victim of the goddess' manipulation? In the *Odyssey*, when Odysseus' son visits the house of Menelaos, where after the victory over the Trojans Helen has been restored as his wife, she drugs the banqueters with nepenthe, an Egyptian drug that takes away pain. And she claims to have been loyal to the Greeks even as she lived in the fortress of Troy; she recognised Odysseus when he crept into the city, disguised as a slave. She swore not to betray him, as she dreamt of returning home to Greece and repented the day when Aphrodite took her away from her husband, her marriage bed, her child.

Menelaos immediately undercuts the pathos of this scene, though, as he recalls how, when the Greeks entered the city of Troy enclosed in the huge wooden horse, Helen walked around it three times and called by name the Greek warriors hidden inside. She imitated their wives' voices, and the fighters within were stricken by waves of longing, to answer her. Odysseus prevented them from speaking out and thwarting the plan of the Greeks to lie in wait inside the horse until the Trojans had celebrated their victory, their breaking of the siege, and night had come. The Greeks, who had feigned departure from Troy, emerged from the belly of the horse, slaughtered the sleeping Trojans, took possession of their women as slaves and brought down their enemies.

So, was Helen responsible for her actions and their consequences? The question continued to preoccupy the Greeks, as in Stesikhoros' first poem, in Alkaios, in later works of the classical period, tragedies in Athens, rhetorical speeches. Sappho here takes a position counter to that of her contemporary Alkaios. If some agent, some force – the goddess, eros himself, itself, her own desire – turned her away from her home, Helen is not condemned, but rather used here as part of a proof, a proof that whatever one loves is the most beautiful thing on the black earth. For Helen, the unstated fact is that Paris/Alexandros, Trojan son of King Priam, was the most beautiful thing on the dark earth, because she loved him.

The poem moves then from this mythic, legendary case, the proof from example, to the situation of the poet herself, speaking in her own voice, as if overheard. She is put in mind, by something – the memory of Helen, Helen herself – of Anaktoria. The woman, the girl, is *ou pareoisas*, 'not present'. In a characteristic move, Sappho alters the temporal landscape of the poem. In fragment 1, the appearance of the goddess Aphrodite belongs to a past that justifies a prayer in the present; Aphrodite is asked to behave as she did before, perhaps often before. Here the remote past, the time of the Trojan war and its aftermath, serves as a paradigm for Sappho's recollection of another sort of past, when Anaktoria was there with her. She has been reminded of Anaktoria through the recounting of Helen's act, and we cannot know if the abandoning of family is stressed because it emphasises the radical, extreme nature of Helen's departure, in a world in which family is the most significant source of the meaning of women's lives, or if it refers somehow to the relationship between the speaking voice and the object of desire, Anaktoria.

Helen left her family, was absent to them; Anaktoria is absent, who once was there. And the voice in the poem moves on to reflect on her longing for this woman. The language of this last, almost complete stanza echoes words used earlier in the poem. The poet says she would rather see the lovely *bama*, 'step', 'pace', using the same root as the verb *eba*, 'went', as in 'went sailing off towards Troy'. Her step is 'lovely', *eraton*, using the same root as the word *eratai*, 'loves', the last word, the verb in the first stanza. And (she would rather see) the radiant *amarukhma*, that is, the sparkle, the twinkle, the quick motion of Anaktoria's face, her look, and here, vividly, Sappho brings the woman into the poem, present, radiant, in motion. She would rather look upon these, Anaktoria's step, her face, and she calls them up in the absence of the woman herself, in longing. They are compared then, as 'whatever one loves', whatever the poet loves, whatever Sappho loves, compared to things that bring us back to the beginning of the poem. She compares the step and face of Anaktoria to the chariots of the Lydians, and to foot soldiers in their armour.

The array of soldiers circles back, then, to the first lines of the poem, in which she says that 'some say an army of horsemen, some of foot soldiers, some of ships to be the most beautiful thing on the black earth'. These cavaliers, these infantrymen, then, return and are rejected in the name of the woman Anaktoria, what Sappho loves. Sappho's preference turns away from admiration of these forces of war, the armies and navies of Homer and of her own world, to choose her lover. Can we read this as a woman's choice, one that sees the violence and blood that come in the wake of chariots, infantrymen and warships, and prefers eros? Sappho may be, as a woman, choosing love over war. And she puts herself in the place of Helen, risking all, family, husband, parents, child, for the sake of eros and aligning herself not with the cultural conventions of the family but with the paradigmatic female lover, Helen, whom she rehabilitates by identifying with in the poem.

And beyond this, in her proto-philosophical gesture, she lays out a definition that prefigures Plato's efforts at definition, at refining and examining language. She both precedes Plato and takes a different position from his. If Socrates is shown over and over in Plato's dialogues, written in the fourth century BCE, trying to cross-examine and refine the language used in everyday life, to clarify and render wise the words men use, Sappho is doing the same thing here, trying to define what is 'the most beautiful'. But rather than moving to a metaphysical plane, as Plato does, arguing that the most beautiful is beauty itself, that it resides, abstractly, above material human experience, in an immaterial, ideal, eternal domain, Sappho chooses the body, the material presence of her beloved. She focuses not even on 'one's lover', 'the person one loves', but rather on one specific human being, named, alive, the one person, the one woman whom she loves. If one of the criticisms of Plato and his philosophical works, and even of the Christian theology that follows upon it, has been that he uses love, the love of particular human beings, as a stepping stone beyond them, to love of the abstract good, then Sappho gives us another way of understanding love, not a generalised and undifferentiated and abstract love of the beautiful and the good, but love for one beloved.

The erotic world of antiquity provides an important context for 'understanding' Sappho. In the world she inhabited, same-sex desire was taken for granted, and many poets wrote about it. Since we have only the barest shreds of the works of other women poets, we know less about female same-sex desire than about men's, but it may be that, especially in the aristocratic circles of archaic cities, men and women's desire for members of their own gender was central to social life. The history of ancient sexuality has been a vexed topic in recent years, with some controversy and scholarly conflict. There is more material to support different points of view in the records from the classical periods of Greece and Rome, and scholars have mined these to prove both that homoeroticism was the norm and that it was disapproved of by some. I will discuss these issues more fully in Chapter 5, but will just bring up a few points for now. There is some mockery, in the comic drama of Aristophanes, of grown men still in thrall to boys, or of the assumption of what was considered an effeminate or slavish passivity in sexual behaviour. Yet the military culture of the classical period assumes male–male desire; some ancient authors point to groups of soldiers in Thebes and elsewhere, formed of pairs of lovers, because it was thought that in battle lovers fought more bravely side by side.

The dialogues of Plato reflect a world of homoerotic pleasure; the author is concerned to deploy the desire men feel for each other in a philosophical project, to move pleasure beyond the body towards abstract beauty and the good. One speaker describes the laws related to eros, and says that in Elis and Boeotia 'it is right for the lover to have his way'. This is so older men will not have to plead with young men for their favours. Although we know less about women's desire for one another in the classical period, in a famous passage in this dialogue, set in a symposium, a drinking party, a speaker describes the origins of desire. He tells the story of three original beings, with two sets of genitals, one on each side of a round body; one of these creatures has two sets of female genitals, one two sets of male members, one both male and female. Zeus was threatened by their agility, their rounded form that sought to reach Olympus. So the great god cut them all in half, and each half was left with a desperate longing for its lost other half, two thirds of the beings longing for their own gender, only a third longing for the 'opposite' sex, and that longing resulting in reproduction.

Before the classical period, the fifth and fourth centuries BCE, in Athens, we have a great deal of evidence concerning male–male desire. There are graffiti from the island of Crete alluding to intercourse between men and later descriptions of the abduction of boys by their older lovers. Male–male sexual intercourse may have been part of initiation into manhood and into military service by citizens of many different city-states. Certainly the poetry of the archaic age, Sappho's time, both before and after her life, stresses the fluid desire of the male poets, who seem to be attracted to beauty, to boys, to men, as well to women, some of whom, those from Lesbos, for example, shun them. Especially in the songs sung at drinking parties, the symposia, which were occasions for aristocratic bonding, men's courtship of boys and initiation into powerful groups in the city, male homoerotic poetry dominates. In visual art, in vase painting and elsewhere, male–male desire is depicted. The painting of the Tomb of the Diver, a beautiful fifth-century BCE representation of a symposium found in Paestum, in southern Italy, depicts two male lovers, shown reclining side by side, with the older bearded man, the *erastes*, pursing his lips and about to kiss his younger beloved, his *eromenos*.

The mention of the Lydians opens another crucial dimension of our understanding of Sappho of Lesbos. Her island lies very near to the coast of Asia. It is the largest of the Aegean islands, in the eastern part of the Mediterranean Sea, offshore from Anatolia, now Turkey. The Greek-speaking population of the several city-states on the island may have been settled by colonists from further west, perhaps Thessaly, a northern region, and Boeotia, south of Thessaly, site of the legendary city of Thebes, home of Oidipous/Oedipus. The Aiolian dialect of Sappho and Alkaios suggests that there were links to these regions in mainland Greece, but the nearness to Asia meant that there were also ties to Anatolia, ties that archaeologists have shown go back beyond the time, probably in the tenth century BCE, when the Aiolian colonists arrived on the island. Early artefacts, such as vases, ceramic fragments and structural remains discovered on the island, and even the gods worshipped there, show features distinct from those on mainland Greece. More of this will be discussed when I consider the question of polytheism in relation to our understanding of Sappho; I want here to stress the ways in which the Lesbians, and Sappho in particular, may have seen themselves as closely bound up with life across the narrow strait between their island and the continent of Asia.

In fragment 16, Sappho compares the lovely step and shining face of Anaktoria to the chariots of the Lydians. The inhabitants of Lydia, on the mainland of Asia, lived in a kingdom rather than an aristocracy or a tyranny such as that of Lesbos and other Greek cities of the islands, and even some sprinkled along the western coast of Asia. These cities were founded in the great period of colonisation by the mainland Greeks when their own cities were overrun by invaders, or when they became overcrowded with burgeoning populations. The Greeks established colonies throughout the

Mediterranean world, along the coasts of western Asia and north Africa, including Egypt, into the Black Sea, further west in what became known as Magna Graecia (on the mainland of southern Italy), on the island of Sicily, in what is now France and even further west. The Lydians of western Asia loomed large in the imagination of the Greeks. Their principal city, Sardis, lay on an important trade route between the Near East and the Aegean sea. They were said to be fabulously wealthy, in part because a natural alloy of gold and silver, electrum, flowed down the river Pactolus from Mt Tmolus. The ancient historian Herodotos recounts that the Lydians invented coinage; numismatists, scholars who work on questions of money and coins, place the invention in the mid-seventh century BCE, around the time of Sappho. Coins may have originally been produced as tokens celebrating the power of the rulers of Lydia, later the Greek cities of Asia Minor and eventually all the Greek world. They became universal equivalents, allowing for a radical transformation of the forms of barter and exchange that had characterised economic life before this achievement.

The Lydians had close ties with the Greek world. Greek colonies dotted the coast of Asia Minor near them, they adopted the Greek alphabet with which to write their language and they made offerings to Greek gods, in the wealthy pan-Hellenic sanctuaries such as Delphi, site of the oracle of Apollo. The kings of Lydia attempted to expand their territory and to conquer the Greek cities, using the chariots and warriors Sappho mentions. Kroisos, ruler of the Lydians after the life of Sappho, went down in history as the most fabulously wealthy man of all time. According to Herodotos, he sent extravagant gifts to Delphi, including the statue of a lion made of pure gold, resting on 117 gold ingots. He sent huge vats of gold and silver, jugs of silver and a statue, 4½ feet high, of a woman said to be the king's baker, a shield of pure gold and a pure gold spear. He consulted the Delphic oracle, which ambiguously predicted the fall of an empire. Overjoyed, Kroisos thought it was the Persian Empire that was doomed; in fact it was his own, and the Persians took control of Lydia. But as he had made rich offerings to the god Apollo at Delphi, the god allegedly saved him from being burnt alive on a pyre by the Persians; Apollo sent a rain that quenched the fire. The fabulous wealth, downfall and rescue of the last of the Lydian kings became legendary.

Although these events took place shortly after the time of Sappho, even in her world Lydia and Sardis, very near to Lesbos, were seen as sites of great luxury and extravagance. Sappho frequently mentions Lydia and its wealth in the surviving fragments. In fragment 132, preserved in a handbook on poetic metre, Hephaistion records this 'procatalectic trochaic' of Sappho:

> I have a beautiful girl, who has the form of golden flowers, beloved Kleis,
> and in her place I would not [take] all of Lydia, or ... lovely

It's not clear from this fragment if Sappho refers to her own daughter, or to a slave child/girl/woman, since the word *pais* is commonly used both for child and slave. The idea of trading, bartering, though, may give weight to the notion that this is a beautiful slave; Sappho would not exchange the vast wealth of all (*paisan*) Lydia for the girl.

Fragment 39 comes from a commentary on a verse of the Athenian comedy writer Aristophanes, which says that Lydian dyes are the best and cites Sappho: 'an elaborate (*poikilos*) leather thong covered her feet, beautiful Lydian handiwork.' In a world far less furnished with exotic commodities than our own, such an object was rare and precious, connoting connections with the nearby Asian continent. In fragment 98 there is the mention of a *poikilan mitranan*, a decorated headband from Sardis, compared, perhaps unfavourably, to garlands, crowns of flowers in hair yellower than a torch. Fragment 101, from the text of Athenaeus, mentions cloths, ornaments for the head, that come from Phocaea, the northernmost part of Greek Asia Minor; the poet calls them 'costly gifts'. But the most magnificent of Sappho's poems mentioning Lydia is fragment 96, from a sixth-century CE parchment. As a fragment, it begins with an enigmatic reference to Lydia's capital:

> Sardis,
> ever mindful of this place.
>
> You – recognized, like a goddess –
> most of all she took delight
> in your dancing song.

How she shines among those Lydian women,
as the sun plunging down,
the rose-fingered moon

surpasses all the stars.
Her light reaches across the salt sea
to the *mille fiori* of the fields.

A lovely dew is poured out,
roses bloom with delicate chervil
and the flowering honey lotus.

Ever wandering, she remembers
dear Atthis, with desire.
She devours her own fine heart.

In the beautiful translation of the poems of Sappho by Mary Barnard, influenced by the great American poet Ezra Pound and first published in 1958, this poem is strangely given a title, imposed on it by twentieth-century editors who invented a context for it. It is called 'To an army wife, in Sardis'. This is a strange projection, in the post-World War II world, into the sixth century BCE. In fact, nothing in the poem would lead the listener or reader to imagine 'an army wife' taken from the company of Sappho and Atthis, another woman, to Lydia. And although there have been centuries of speculation about the relationship among these women, all we have is the poem itself.

The word Sardis can be teased out of the papyrus, but nothing of its context, the words that surround it. Somehow, the Lydian capital figures in the beginning of the fragment. Then a female person's mind turns often in this direction, that is, towards the singer and the person she is addressing. And the poet's voice uses the second person, 'you', to describe the relationship of that absent one to this present one. There is some doubt of what follows here; is the word *arignotai* a name, Arignota, or an adjective describing her, meaning 'well-known/renowned'? If this is the name of another woman, then the poem contains references to the absent woman in Sardis, an Arignota, and Atthis, a third woman, companion somehow of the poet. 'You' were comparable to a well-known goddess. This clause echoes one in the *Odyssey*, in which the poet compares the young girl Nausikaa to Artemis, virgin goddess of the hunt; Odysseus will encounter her as he emerges, rough, naked from a night's sleep after shipwreck, and again say she is nearest to Artemis in her grace and beauty. The allusion stresses the youth and perfection of the woman in Sappho's poem, praised by the absent woman in Sardis in this elegant allusion to Homer. That distant woman also delighted most in the song of Sappho's companion.

After these references to a past of admiration and shared presence, the poem goes on to compliment the woman in Sardis in an extended simile, a long comparison, which uses this literary device so often found in the verses of Homer. The *Iliad* and the *Odyssey* often expand a scene of immediate description with a simile that draws in another world, sometimes a pastoral or rural scene, some timeless moment that opens up the epics in unexpected ways. The blood dripping from a wound is likened to the crimson dye used to stain an ivory ornament for a horse; a warrior falling in battle is like a great tree crashing to the forest floor. In the *Odyssey* the singer compares Penelope, united with her long-lost husband, rejoicing, to a shipwrecked swimmer at last washed up on the sun-warmed shore. Here Sappho uses this mode, of 'likening', to imagine the distant beloved woman, bringing her near, into the space of the poem.

Among the Lydian women, the women, perhaps, of Sardis, she is pre-eminent, conspicuous, and here too there may be a gesture towards the girl Nausikaa, who shines among her companions like Artemis among her nymphs. And Artemis is there called *arignota*, 'easily recognised', though all her companions are beautiful, and Nausikaa is said to *meteprepe*, to 'stand out', a word sharing the root *prepo* in *emprepetai*, 'is conspicuous', 'shines out', in Sappho's poem. The woman, among the Lydians now, is compared to the moon, and the poet uses an unusual adjective for that heavenly body. Homer calls the dawn 'rosy-fingered' and we can picture the first rays of light appearing at the dark eastern horizon of the earth as the sun rises. But Sappho turns this scene, this reference to the beginning of day, and calls the moon 'rose-fingered'. Roses, of course, come in many colours, red, pink, golden, even white, and perhaps the reference is to the silvery aura of the moon. Even more significant, however, is Sappho's rewriting, turning, of the Homeric allusion to dawn, her finding beauty in the night, in sunset, as the sun sinks in the west. This woman now resides in the East, in Asia, but is likened to the silvery moon that surpasses all the stars, just as she surpasses all the Lydian women.

The simile extends to the next two stanzas; the light of the moon reaches out to the salty sea, just as to the many-flowered fields. The light of the moon brings together Sappho and her interlocutor, her audience, on the island, across the sea to the land of Asia. The salt sea is sterile, not productive of crops. The word *arourais*, arable land, tilled land, that is, fields, suggests the analogy made by the Greeks in marital contexts, in which the body of the bride is likened to the fertile fields of the city. She is meant to be ploughed by her husband, who will plant in her furrow the seed of the next generation; women and the city's fields bring forth crops for the perpetuation of the city. The language and the rituals of this world pursue this analogy; even Oidipous, in his anguish at having impregnated his own mother, speaks of the 'twice-ploughed field', *diplen arouran*, of Iokasta, which yielded both himself and his children. These fields of Sappho are remarkable because they bring forth not the children or the sustaining grains of the classical city, but flowers. These *mille fiori*, blooming in the moonlight, bespeak luxury and pleasure rather than the reproductive tasks of ploughing and sowing and harvesting.

The moon brings to light the flowering fields as well as the salt sea, and seems to fertilise those fields. The next stanza portrays the dew poured out, flowing, streaming in beauty. The word *eersa*, 'dew', means dew, in the plural raindrops, and metaphorically a young and tender thing, such as a lamb born late in the season. It has an analogue in Sanskrit, the ancient language of India, in *varsham*, which means 'rain'. In the *Iliad*, in a scene cited earlier, the seduction of Zeus by Hera, wearing Aphrodite's belt, their love-making causes glistening dewdrops to fall. The dew falls from heaven, from cloud-gatherer Zeus, from the intercourse of the two great gods; in Sappho's poem, it pours out, seemingly from the moon, on the fields of flowers. And Sappho names them: roses, chervil and honey lotus. The roses have bloomed, in the perfect tense, and therefore are blooming; the chervil is tender and delicate; and the melilot, the honey lotus is flowery, *anthemodes*, a word that echoes the adjective used of the fields, the 'many-flowered', *poluanthemois*, fields. Luxuriant, ephemeral, aromatic flowers somehow here seem to defy the command to reproduce, to produce food for the city, and insist on pleasure, adornment and perhaps an aristocratic, even Lydian, Asiatic way of being that will be often repudiated in the more austere world of the classical *polis*. In other poems of Sappho, as we will see, flowers are the signifiers of eros and feminine community.

After this extended simile, the poem concludes with a portrait of the absent one, the woman pre-eminent among the Lydians. She is roaming, wandering, going back and forth, many times, seemingly restlessly searching. And she is remembering as she goes, remembering gentle Atthis *imero*, 'with desire', 'with longing', 'with yearning'. The last words of this stanza, which may be the last lines of the poem itself, although this is disputed, are very difficult to decipher because of the fragmentary nature of the papyrus. Different editors have produced different solutions to the problem. One of the most difficult words is *boretai*, which here may say, may mean, 'eats', or 'is eaten', or 'feeds itself'. The word *bora*, root of the verb, means 'food', usually of carnivorous animals, so it implies a kind of violence here. The line seems to say something like: 'She is eaten, with respect to her tender heart, because of your "fate".' This last word in the English, too, is illegible on the papyrus, and has been supplied as *kari*, also problematic. *Ker* is goddess of death or doom; she appears, sometimes in the plural, the Keres, in Homer on numerous occasions. Hephaistos, forging the shield of Akhilleus at his mother's request, in a divine act of creation, shows a battle like that of the *Iliad*'s, and on it appears *oloe Ker*, 'deadly Fate', dragging dead men through the battle fray, around her shoulders a garment red with men's blood. So if this is the correct reading, what is the fate, the doom, the *ker* of the one remembered? Is Sappho addressing someone dead, or gone, recalling another woman now absent in Sardis?

Like other poems of Sappho's corpus, this fragment plays with distance and with time. Often an addressee, even the goddess Aphrodite, is distant, absent, and is called into the presence of the singer. Often that singer recalls the past presence of a loved one with regret and yearning. And the time, the temporality of the poems is not fixed; the past is present, the future summoned and the voice of the poem orchestrates these complexities with great elegance. Aphrodite is summoned, was once present, vividly, and is recalled, in fragment 1. In fragment 96, less well preserved, there is a similar play of elements of recollection, the imagination of someone far away and a sense of yearning that defines the present of the poet's performance. Fragment 96, directed eastwards, towards Asia and an Asiatic luxuriousness later called into question by the democratic practices of the classical Athenians, takes pleasure and pain from the experience of recollection.

In fragment 94, another long piece, we find again a scene of intense exchange and an atmosphere of sensuality and erotic pleasure that illuminates fragment 96, and which again turns the audience, the listener, the reader, towards an exotic East.

> I wish I were dead! Literally. Dead.
> She was weeping. She was going away from me.
>
> Over and over she then said to me:
> 'Oh how sublime, what we have experienced,
> Sappho. And yet I am forced to leave you behind.'
>
> And I could only reply by saying these things:
> 'Farewell. Go now, and remember
> me. For you know how much we cared for you,
>
> and if not, well, that's why I want
> to remind you ......
> ...... and those beautiful things we felt.
>
> For the many crowns of violets
> and roses and of crocuses intertwined,
> ...... you put around yourself at my side,

and the many garlands woven from
flowers ......
circling your delicate neck

and with so much ...... fragrant oil,
precious ...... queenly ...
you anointed yourself.

And on soft beds
for your tender ......
you would satisfy your desire ...

and there was no ... nor any
sacred place ......
from which we were absent.

No grove ...... no dance
... sound ...

Fragment 94 is the most sexually explicit of the longer poems. Like others of the works of Sappho, this poem works through a complex network of references to companions, to absence, and to the pleasures of the past, in a vividly realised recollection.

This poem, or what we have of it, begins in the middle of something: someone wishes she were dead, in the first person. The first line is a stark statement. It uses a word, *adolos*, 'artlessly', 'without fraud', containing the same root, *dolos*, 'craft', 'cunning', 'deceit', that Sappho used to describe Aphrodite, *doloploke*, 'weaver of deceit', in fragment 1. The voice in fragment 94 speaks without cunning, artlessly, honestly, of a desire to die. Possibly a hyberbolic statement, exaggerated in the mode of ordinary conversation, but also possibly a sign of these women's inability to control their own destinies. Is the 'author' of this poem wishing to be dead, or is it someone else, who spoke to that author, in the past? The woman was weeping, and leaving, and then she is quoted directly, reminding

'Sappho', or the character in the intimate conversation in the poem, of their shared past.

The speaker, contained within the performance of the poem, expresses dismay and exclaims about what *deina*, 'what terrible things, or what marvellous things, or what strange things', they have experienced together. The verb *peponthamen*, in the perfect tense, in past time, can mean 'we had suffered', in a neutral sense, that is, what has happened to us. It doesn't necessarily imply pain and suffering, just the passivity of experience, of enduring. The speaker addresses Sappho directly, calling her by name, in the same place at the beginning of the line of verse as the address by Aphrodite in fragment 1. In this poem, the scene, set in the past, takes on a similar immediacy with the recollection of this use of the poet's name in what is called the vocative, the grammatical case of direct address. This woman is leaving Sappho *aekoisa*, 'unwillingly', 'against her will'.

And now Sappho recalls her own words at this scene of separation. If the poem begins with someone using the first person singular, 'I', it then moves to 'we', and now Sappho speaks as an 'I'. In the past, she spoke to the departing woman, giving her a conventional farewell, asking to be remembered and then reminding her of their shared past. The poem builds a complex network of persons, first-person singular, the 'I'; second-person singular, the case of direct address, 'you'; first-person plural, 'we'. If these two were to be parted, they have a past, a past shared with others as well. Sappho reminds her friend, her lover, of how 'we cherished you', *pedepomen*, which connotes, as well as care, a sense of pursuit, of following. Others are drawn into the circle with this first-person plural.

And if this woman does not know, Sappho wishes to remind her, echoing with *thelo*, 'I wish', the first line of this fragment. Some of what follows is illegible, but she then counters the departing woman's words, *deina peponthamen*, which, as noted, could be understood as 'what terrible things we suffered'. Sappho proposes, in their place, 'the beautiful things we used to experience', using the same verb but in the imperfect, a continuous past tense rather than the perfect. The poem goes on to recreate the atmosphere of lush, erotically charged, beautiful experiences once shared, and again flowers, their ephemeral, scented beauty, contribute to the scene. The addressee, the woman addressed, now gone, is reminded of how she put on many encircling crowns of violets and roses and crocuses, alongside Sappho. Around her delicate neck she placed garlands, woven and made from flowers. In a further elaboration of this elegant, voluptuous scene, Sappho recalls the aromatic scents she used on her body, and here again we find reference to the luxurious commodities associated with Asia, with the nearby land to the east of Lesbos. She anointed herself with sweet oil, like that used by Hera in the *Iliad* in her seduction of Zeus. The word *muron*, 'perfume', 'balsam', occurs elsewhere in the lyric poets earlier than or contemporary with Sappho, and is associated with sexual attraction and pleasure.

In his encyclopedic work the *Learned Banqueters*, Athenaeus, the Egyptian writer of the second and third centuries CE, makes clear the importance of crowns, garlands and perfumes to the festive banquets of antiquity. The seventh-century BCE poet Arkhilokhos alludes to *muron*, saying that some women displayed their scented hair and breasts so that even old men would fall in love with them. Athenaeus says that Arkhilokhos is the first poet to use the word *muron*, 'perfume'. He further suggests that the word *muron* is derived from *murrha*, 'myrrh', gum from an Arabian tree, as many perfumes, *mura*, are made with myrrh. Anakreon, a poet who seems to have lived slightly later than Sappho, through the sixth century BCE, calls on someone to anoint his chest with *muron*, to soothe his heart and hasten to his side. The word *brentheio*, perhaps meaning 'expensive', 'costly', occurs only here in the remaining texts from antiquity, in Sappho's verse and in the work of Pherekrates, a writer of comedies, playwright in Athens in the fifth century BCE. Some scholars believe that the word suggests expense because the scented oil concerned was made of some specific flower. In Sappho's poem, the costly oil is *basileio*, 'royal/queenly/fit for a queen'.

The addressee of this poem anointed herself with this costly, queenly oil, a seductive perfume. And then, in the most explicit of phrases, Sappho describes an erotic scene. 'On soft beds, you would satisfy your longing.' The phrase *exies pothon*, 'you put away your desire', is used elsewhere for satisfying other appetites: in the *Iliad*, Homer uses the expression, 'they put away their desire, *eros*, for drink and food'. Here in Sappho's fragmentary verse, the *pothos*, 'longing/yearning', is for something *apalan*, 'delicate', echoing the word used of the woman's neck in the earlier stanza.

This passage has excited some controversy in the past, although it seems clear that more than hunger and thirst were being satisfied on the soft beds of Lesbos. For one thing, the word used for beds here, *stromnan*, means something 'spread out', 'beds/mattresses/bedding', possibly to be distinguished from the bench, couch, on which one customarily reclined or sat to eat and drink. But the great twentieth-century editor of the Greek lyric poets, Denys Page, was uncomfortable with the likely connotations of these lines for the reputation of Sappho. Like others who wrote about Sappho as late as the twentieth century, Page made a valiant effort to rescue her from the homophobic accusations of deviancy and perversion that will be discussed in later chapters of this book. He wrote cautiously in *Sappho and Alcaeus* in 1955, after acknowledging the 'lover's passion' expressed in Sappho's poems, in response to the question of whether she acted on her desires, that 'a negative answer must be returned' (p. 144).

The poem as we have it ends with a haunting, fragmentary list of memories. The poet's voice represents both presence and absence, as before, saying that there was 'no ... no shrine, from which we were absent, no grove, no dance ...' The complex expression through the negative, citing presence through the negation of absence, 'we were not absent', characteristically underlines the play between memory, past and present, presence and absence. The elements of ritual, the shrine, the grove, the dance, create the shadow of occasions of celebration. Worship of the goddess, of goddesses, and of gods, took place in sacred sanctuaries, in holy groves, with choruses of dancers and singers performing in honour of the divinities. So the satisfying of desire on soft beds took place, once upon a time, along with collective celebration of the gods. And the return to the first-person plural here, 'we', impossibly restores a lost whole, a community of desire and worship, from which the absent woman is now cut off, present to the others only through memory and the longing expressed in this song. In fragment 126, Sappho sends a wish to another addressee: 'may you lie sleeping on the breast of your tender companion.'

Before looking at other poems in which Sappho alludes to the luxury and beauty associated with Lydia and with the gaze east towards Asia, I want to call up another of the fragments, one which illuminates the setting of shrine, grove and dance hauntingly recalled in fragment 94 in the context of the satisfaction of desire, of flowers and perfumes. This is fragment 2, the summoning of the goddess Aphrodite, again with song, this time in a more formal, less supplicatory mode than that of fragment 1:

> Come here to me from Crete to this sacred temple,
> where exists your delightful grove
> of apple trees and altars smoking
>   with frankincense.
>
> And in it, a cold spring sounds through apple boughs,
> and the whole place is veiled with roses,
> and from their trembling petals
>   enchanted sleep drops.
>
> And in it, a horse-grazing meadow blooms
> with spring blossoms, and the winds
> gently breathe ...
>
> There you, Kypris, take ...
> in golden wine cups,
> luxuriously mixed with our festivities,
>   nectar pour.

Here the speaker summons the goddess not from her father's house on Olympus, but from Crete. This poem has had an extraordinary history. The Italian classicist Medea Norsa found it on a broken piece of pottery and published it in 1937. It is full of dictation errors, and some scholars have speculated that it was a student's copy, made on the waste paper of antiquity, a broken ceramic shard.

    The goddess is called from the island of Crete, whose inhabitants claimed that they were the first to worship Aphrodite, born according to some accounts, as explained earlier, in the sea from sea foam, from the fragments of her father's castration. She was worshipped at the city of Knossos on Crete as 'Aphrodite Antheia', Aphrodite of the blossoms. Elsewhere she was said to have washed up at Paphos on Cyprus, that is, on the easternmost of the islands, and later in this poem Sappho calls her 'Kypris', the Cyprian, one of the names the Greeks used for the goddess. Scholars have remarked on the incantatory quality of this poem, its hypnotic mood, as if the song itself could bring the goddess to the site. The grove has altars smoking with incense, *libanoto*, 'frankincense', another of the aromatic substances associated with Asia. The fifth-century BCE historian Herodotos describes the harvesting of frankincense and other aromatic substances, in Arabia. The Arabians collect frankincense, myrrh and cinnamon; to gather frankincense, they first produce smoke to drive off flying snakes that guard the frankincense trees. (Another sweet-smelling aromatic substance can be obtained only by unsticking it from the beards of male goats which have been grazing among the bushes that produce it.) The exoticism of these perfumes, their origin in Arabia, add to their value and to their potency in erotic play, and in the summoning of the divinities in acts of worship and sacrifice.

In Sappho's grove, cool water babbles through the apple branches, the whole place is shaded by roses and from the shimmering leaves *koma*, a 'trance', a sleep induced by enchantment, pours down. In Greek, the sounds, echoing one another, produce a hypnotic effect. The repetition, for example, of the letters k, *kappa*, and kh, *chi*, gather to a rhythmic, soothing pulse: *psukhron, keladei, khoros, eskiast', koma katerrei*, 'enchanted sleep comes down'. In translation, it is, as I will discuss in Chapter 4, difficult to replicate this play of alliteration, of the repetition of initial sounds, and of internal rhymes and echoes. But the song itself seems to aim at producing an enchanted sleep in the listener, even as the goddess is summoned from afar.

The scene includes not just this grove of babbling brook, apples, roses and entrancing sleep, but also a meadow, often in Greek lyric a site of erotic play. Here horses graze, and spring flowers blossom, and winds blow gently. As the listeners are soothed, enchanted, drawn to this beautiful, perfect, idyllic and holy space, sacred to the goddess Aphrodite, she is addressed again directly, this time she herself imagined already there. And again, the prayer, the request, assumes the goddess' goodwill and benign response, as the supplicant asks her to pour, that is, to 'wine-pour', *oinokhoaison*, into gold cups the nectar that is mixed with the company's festivities. The golden cups signify the opulence of their celebration. The Cyprian one, Aphrodite, is asked to pour *abros*, 'luxuriously', 'gracefully', a word associated later with an Asian, aristocratic, almost decadent way of life that is condemned by a more austere and levelling Athenian democracy. The drink is *nektar*, 'nectar', the beverage of the gods, associated with the food of those gods, ambrosia, a word that means immortality, 'not-mortality', existence not subject to death. Aphrodite is asked to pour out this drink of the divinities, to share it, or to drink along with the celebrants, wine-drinking mortals. In a citation of these last lines, the later writer Athenaeus adds the phrase 'for these my friends and yours', in a gesture that incorporates a collectivity into the celebration, companions of the singer and of the goddess herself.

If this arrival of the goddess, the Cyprian one, is requested from the island of Crete, there are other signs, in other poems or songs, in which the situation of Sappho, on her island near Lydia, faces eastwards rather than towards the population centres of the Greek mainland, the homelands from which colonising Greeks departed, the city of Athens which was to become the cultural centre of the ancient Greek world in the fifth and fourth centuries BCE. Even the worship of Aphrodite had its sources, in all probability, in the East. Scholars connect the goddess with the ancient Mesopotamian divinities of fertility, love and war such as Inanna, Ishtar and Astarte. Tremendously powerful in the stages of culture preceding the Bronze Age, they were still worshipped, among many other divinities, in subsequent centuries, and we find mention of Asherah, for example, in the Hebrew Bible. Aphrodite seems to be related to these goddesses, who oversaw fertility and reproduction; on the island of Crete were found images of a 'Mistress of the Animals'. The Greek divinities Artemis, virgin goddess of the hunt and of wild animals, and Aphrodite, voluptuous divinity of erotic desire and reproduction, together carry on the legacy of these eastern divinities.

One sign of the continuity between the goddesses of Mesopotamia, Asia Minor, Canaan and Israel is the celebration of the feast of Adonis. In the Greek story, Myrrha, later turned into the myrrh tree, gave birth to Adonis after incest with her father Kinyras. The beautiful young man attracted the attention of Aphrodite, who tried to keep him safe by hiding him in a chest and giving it to Persephone; this queen of the underworld refused to let him go. Zeus commanded that the beautiful young man spend four months each year in Hades, and four months with Aphrodite. According to some versions of the story, she begged him not to go on a hunting expedition, but he defied her and was killed, gored by a wild boar. The goddess mourned. In a festival later celebrated in Athens, in the African-Egyptian-Macedonian-Greek city of Alexandria, and in Byblos, in Phoenicia, now Lebanon, his untimely death was lamented. The Athenian rite involved women planting seeds in the heat of the summer and then mourning their withering. The whole population of Byblos wept and lamented, but then celebrated the young man's resurrection. The Semitic name Adon means 'lord'; Adonis was related to the eastern mythic figures: Sumerian Dumuzi, lover of Inanna/Ishtar, Babylonian Tammuz and the Canaanite god Baal. And we find mention of Adonis in Sappho's verses.

The name of Adonis appears in the broken lines at the end of Sappho's fragment 96, which begins with the name of the Lydian city Sardis. Hephaistion, author of the treatise on metre mentioned earlier as a source for some of Sappho's fragments, uses these Sapphic lines from fragment 140:

> He is dying, o Cytherea, delicate Adonis; what shall we do?
> Beat your breasts, girls, and rip your clothes.

This may be an exchange between the celebrants of the Adoneia ritual and the goddess Aphrodite, here called Cytherea, because of her association with the island of Cythera, an alternative site of her birth. In the second-century BCE *Art of Grammar*, another reader of Sappho, Dionysios Thrax, cites a verse: 'O Adonis', a cry of lamentation. In the later collection of poems called the *Palatine Anthology*, one Dioskorides writes in honour and praise of his predecessor Sappho, and reminds the reader of her 'mourning with Aphrodite as she grieves for the young son of Kinyras'. This is the poet who calls the songs of Sappho her deathless, her immortal daughters.

*

The ancient sources report that Sappho was married. The *Suda*, the encyclopedia or lexicon compiled in the tenth century CE, says that she married a man named Kerkulas, a trader from the island of Andros, and that they had a daughter called Kleis. Like other elements of her biography, however, these 'facts' are open to question. The name 'Kerkulas of Andros' means 'Mr Prick from the island of Man', and may actually be derived from an obscene joke told by a comic poet, of which more later. And the claim that Sappho had a daughter named Kleis may be based on a poem mentioned earlier, in which she says she has a beautiful child named Kleis. But, as noted before, the word *pais* can mean both child and slave. These ancient biographers, it appears, often developed a life story for characters from the remote past, basing their details on poems which do not necessarily record historical truth. The *Suda* mentions three brothers of Sappho, and three companions and friends, Atthis, Telesippa and Megara, also found in the poems. This entry, about as distant in time from Sappho as the fall of the Roman Empire is from us, also reports that Sappho had a bad reputation because of her shameful, disgraceful love/friendship, *philia*, with these women. This slander too will be looked into more fully later.

The question of Sappho's marriage may be irresolvable, but some of her poems do fit the pattern of what are called *epithalamia*, 'marriage songs'. It is believed that her poems were collected in nine books, most of which are still lost. The books were organised largely in terms of the metres in which the songs were composed, and the ninth book seems to have contained the marriage songs. One of these, fragment 27, from an Egyptian papyrus, asks for favours, 'for we are going to a wedding'. Another is fragment 30, from the same papyrus (the lacunae, the missing parts of the fragment, are marked here in John Daley's translation by double colons):

    Night : :

    Maidens
    celebrating all the night long
    would sing of your love for
        a violet-lapped bride.

> But arise! Go to
> your bachelor comrades, so that
> even less than the clear-voiced nightingale
> will we see sleep.

These choral songs would have been sung, and danced too, by young girls. Another epithalamion, named for the bridal chamber, the thalamus, is fragment 111:

> Hoist high the roof beam
> Hymen, O Hymenaios!
> Raise it up, you builders
> O Hymenaios!
> The bridegroom is arriving equal to Ares
> much bigger than the biggest man.

This fragment gave the American writer J. D. Salinger the title of his *Raise High the Roof-Beam, Carpenters*, published in 1955. Fragment 112 addresses the groom:

> Fortunate bridegroom, the marriage you prayed for
> has come to fruition. You have the maiden for whom you prayed.
> : :   And you, your form is graceful, your eyes
> like honey. Eros pours over your beloved face
> : :   Aphrodite has rewarded you extravagantly.

A bridegroom is compared to a slender sapling in fragment 115; 110a describes the 'door-keeper', who may have served to keep the friends of the bride from rescuing her in the mock abduction that was part of the marriage ritual, as having feet seven fathoms long, wearing sandals made of five oxhides, cobbled by ten cobblers. Athenaeus quotes another poem, listed as fragment 141, in which Sappho is said to portray a marriage feast, perhaps among the gods; ambrosia has been mixed, and the god Hermes took the *krater*, the mixing bowl, and poured out wine for the gods. All held drinking cups, and they offered libations and prayed for good things for the groom. One exceptional find among the papyri, listed as fragment 103, gives the first lines of ten different Sapphic poems, lost to us now, including mention of 'the bride with her beautiful feet'; 'the daughter of Zeus, violet-robed'; 'setting aside anger ... violet-robed'; 'holy Graces and Pierian Muses; hearing a clear-toned song'; 'a bridegroom, disdainful to companions'; 'her hair, setting down the lyre'; 'golden-sandalled Dawn...', all these tantalising and enigmatic still, since no other papyri have been uncovered that give us these texts.

Other fuller fragments concerning the rituals of marriage seem to express regret, or the shock of the great change in a young woman's life, as she married and left the home of her father for that of her husband's family. Fragment 114 directly addresses *parthenia*, 'virginity'.

> Maidenhood, maidenhood, where have you gone abandoning me?
> Never again will I come to you.

Greek thinking on the matter of 'virginity' perhaps differed from that current today, in that the emphasis was not on the loss of the hymen, which was not recognised in medicine, but rather on the age status of a girl, sometimes seen as resembling a wild animal needing, as she entered adolescence, to be tamed and domesticated in marriage.

Another set of fragments, possibly related and listed together as numbers 105a and c, from two different later writers, speaks of the experience of a bride:

> As the sweet apple blushes red upon the highest branch,
> high on the highest branch, where apple harvesters have left it hanging,
> but no, they haven't totally forgotten it, they just couldn't reach there.

And:

> Like a hyacinth in the mountains, sheep-herding men
> use their feet to crush the purple flower into the ground.

The first of these fragments compliments the bride by stressing her remoteness from the ordinary, her height above the rest; the second suggests a violence brought to the natural world of fruits and flowers, as clumsy shepherds, men (*andres*), trample the beauty of the hyacinth. Again, in fragment 107, attributed to Sappho by Apollonius Dyscolus, of the second century CE, someone asks: 'Do I still grasp at virginity (*parthenias*)?'

The once accepted view of Sappho, that she was a schoolmistress, a teacher of girls, chaste, perhaps an 'invert', if not a 'pervert', as one translator put it, has been debunked. It is impossible, though, to establish a firm understanding of what relationship the poet Sappho had with her community. As we have seen, she wrote poetry celebrating weddings; she wrote songs in the first person, the 'I', which portray her desire for women. Other poems draw on a strain of regret, even hostility and pessimism. Fragment 168b goes: 'The moon has gone down, and the Pleiades; it is the middle of the night, time goes by, and I lie alone.' In one line in fragment 146, which has a wonderful alliteration, repetition of the sound of the letter m, *mu*, she says: 'for me neither the honey nor the bee', *mete moi meli mete melissa*, that is, neither sweetness nor the sting. In fragment 131 she complains to the girl Atthis that the thought of Sappho has become hateful, 'and you fly away to Andromeda'. Although she says in fragment 120 that she has a gentle heart, and is not spiteful, there are moments of venom.

One last fragment shows the contempt with which the aristocratic Sappho could condemn another woman, whom she dismisses as a paltry rival, a country girl. This poem, fragment 57, is said to mock Andromeda:

> What rustic bumpkin girl casts a spell over your mind,
> dressed in her rustic clothing,
> not even knowing to drape her robes and cover her ankles.

Urban elegances, finery imported from Asia, these escape the poor country girl. And in fragment 55 Sappho pours scorn on another woman for her lack of education:

> Dead you will lie. And neither will there ever be any memory of you,
> nor any to long afterwards, for you shall have no share of the roses
> from Pieria. But unseen in the House of Hades,
> you also will wander with obscure corpses, having flown away.

The roses of Pieria are the roses of the Muses, inhabitants of the mountain in Macedonia; those deprived of their attentions are ignorant and will be invisible after death. Another poem, another sort of curse, is fragment 37: 'Let the winds, and sorrows, carry away the one who chastises.' Of course, as always in these fragments, we cannot know who is speaking, whether it is the voice of the poet, the character 'Sappho' who, as we have seen, is addressed by others sometimes in the poems, or whether it is another speaker entirely, someone with a place in a surrounding narrative or context that has gone missing.

The most striking example of a hostile poem is fragment 99, which is difficult to read because of its highly broken state. But this poem seems to have the harshness of some other poets of the age, who wrote 'iambic' verse, in a metre used for satire and ridicule by Arkhilokhos and others. Arkhilokhos, who probably lived in the seventh century BCE, used invective and obscenity, and was said to have so deeply humiliated one family that its members hanged themselves. Fragment 99 has been assigned by some scholars to Alkaios, Sappho's contemporary on the island of Lesbos, but she seems to have it in for the family of Polyanax. Maximus of Tyre likens Sappho to Socrates in her use of irony, citing her in a fragment numbered 155: 'I wish the daughter of the house of Polyanax a very good day.' And in fragment 99, Sappho appears to use a word 'of unusual coarseness' that excited indignation and even disbelief in some interpreters:

> ... after a short ... descendants of Polyanax
> strike the lyre strings ... receiving the dildo
> affectionately ... trembles

This is part a; the papyrus continues with what seems to be an address to Apollo, but then again mentions the descendants of Polyanax, and concludes:

'I want to point out the mad one [or the lustful one].' The word translated as 'dildo', *olisbos*, has been variously understood. It has been read as referring to the *plektron*, the instrument for striking the lyre, and some ancient sources attribute the invention of this device to Sappho herself. But the receivers of the *olisbos* seem more likely to be those receiving the dildo, a phallus, usually made of leather, part of the erotic life of the ancient Greeks, along with perfumes and crowns and soft beds. Many later vases show erotic scenes, with dildos either deployed, in action, or hanging on the wall above scenes of sexual intercourse between various partners, or used singly by women. This poem may be invective, insults directed against the descendants of Polyanax, forced to satisfy their desire by mechanical means, but in any case efforts to avoid the sexual connotations of the word seem prudish. The later comic works of Aristophanes, in the fifth century BCE, and of Herodas, in the third century BCE, speak freely of dildos: In Aristophanes' *Lysistrata*, a comedy about Greek women from various cities conducting a sex strike to end the Peloponnesian War of the later fifth century BCE, the heroine Lysistrata complains that because of the war the women can't get imports any more, not even a decent foot-long dildo. Twenty-first-century readers will be more accustomed to, more tolerant of, the mention of sex toys, than classical scholars of the nineteenth and twentieth centuries who, even in the massive and authoritative lexicon of the Greek language, resorted to Latin, '*penis coriaceus*', that is, 'leather penis', when defining the Greek word.

In any case, although in fragment 120 Sappho has claimed a gentle heart for herself, and refused spite, these poems may show a competitive, aggressive side to her poetry. And such manners, of rivalry, jealousy and competition for favours, coincide with the mood of the very first poem, discussed in the preceding chapter, in which she begs Aphrodite to turn the tables on a woman who rejects her, to make her pursue when once she fled.

While many of the fragments discussed thus far concern Sappho's worship of Aphrodite, summoning her to her side, invoking her presence, Sappho lived in a world of many gods. The tendency of modern readers to see only Aphrodite in this landscape may have more to do with our inhabiting a supposedly monotheist religious sphere than with the realities of antiquity.

Whether modern persons, especially in the West, are believers or not, believers in one of the three great monotheisms, Judaism, Christianity and Islam, or not, the institutions of the state and popular culture create a mentality, a mindset, that, for the most part, leads many people to conceive of the divine sphere as inhabited by one god, the god the father. The ancient Greeks saw the world and their gods very differently, and Sappho is no exception.

Theologians have invented the concept of henotheism; in some polytheist cultures, they argue, with many gods, people choose one particular god and focus their worship on this one divinity, even while accepting, acknowledging, even acting on the existence of others. In the greatest polytheist religion of the present, Hinduism, some worshippers do privilege one divinity above others – Vishnu, Shiva, Devi, or one of any number of other divinities. And perhaps because many Westerners have been accustomed to monotheism for many centuries, they may unwittingly tend to see such practices as monotheistic and even to project backwards, onto such societies as ancient Greece, henotheism or even monotheism, understanding Sappho, for example, as a worshipper of Aphrodite.

Some of the divinities Sappho names in her poems are closely associated with Aphrodite. She mentions the Graces and the Muses, and Eros, the personification of sexual desire, the son, the companion of the goddess Aphrodite, who accompanies her and works her will on her victims. Fragment 47 describes the effects of this force, this boy:

> Eros has rattled my heart
> like a mountain wind rushing down on oaks.

This fragment resembles number 48, from Julian, the Roman emperor who sought to re-establish the worship of the pagan gods against the rise of Christianity; he wrote in a letter, citing Sappho: 'You arrived, and I was yearning after you,/ and you cooled my heart that was burning with desire' (translated by John Daley). But in fragment 47, love, desire, eros, Eros, is a being.

Sappho was not a monotheist, not a henotheist, and, like all the poets of her day, if she paid particular attention to the goddess of desire,

Aphrodite, she recognised and acknowledged and addressed other gods as well. Fragment 17, which has features that link it to another recently discovered poem, to be discussed in Chapter 4, is a fragmentary prayer to the goddess Hera:

> Near me, as I pray you that you may appear
> Lady Hera   :   :   your elegant figure
> to whom the sons of Atreus prayed.
>   Those glorious kings
>
> having won many prizes,
> first around Ilium, then on the high sea,
> but then setting out for this place
>   were not able to complete the voyage
>
> until they appealed to you and to Zeus of the supplicants
> and to Thyone's son who excites desire.
> Now be gracious, and help me also
>   in accord with the ancient ways.
>
> Sacred and beautiful   :
> :   maidens
> gather round
>   :   :
>
>   :   :
>   to be   :
>   :   to arrive at the shrine

Like many other poems of this period, including those by Sappho herself, this prayer contains allusions to the epic age, the time of the Trojan war and its heroes. According to local legend, which differs from the received version in Homer's *Odyssey*, the Atreidai, Menelaos and Agamemnon, the sons of Atreus, after their conquest and destruction of Troy sailed back to the

Peloponnesos by way of the island of Lesbos. In the *Odyssey*, Agamemnon and Menelaos have already separated, and the voyagers who stop on Lesbos prayed to Zeus alone. Here Sappho lists not just Hera, the first addressee of her prayer, but Zeus and the entrancing son of Thyone, Dionysos, another great god. In the *Odyssey*, the travellers simply enquire about the best route for sailing back to Hellas. In this fragment they have to overcome some obstacle that prevents them from sailing on, and the three gods together assisted them. This legend may refer to a contrary wind, or a storm that held the fleet at Lesbos.

We know of the shrine of the three gods on the island from other sources. Sappho's contemporary and fellow Lesbian, Alkaios, also wrote about this sacred site. In his fragment 129, from papyrus fragments of the second century CE, he says that the Lesbians established a great and highly visible sanctuary to be held in common, with altars of the immortal and blessed gods. They named Zeus and the god Dionysos, eater of raw flesh. The third divinity named there Alkaios calls 'the Aiolian, renowned mother of all'. The Aiolian may be Hera, although some archaeologists believe that the triple shrine could refer to an Aegean or Asiatic goddess and her companions, and point eastwards, to divinities brought to the island of Lesbos from Asia. More will be said about this fragment of Alkaios in the subsequent section, when I discuss the politics of this period on Lesbos, and also about Alkaios' fragment 130, which mentions the contests held in the precinct of Hera, where the Lesbian women, with trailing robes, competed and were judged for beauty. But it may be that there is some pertinent emphasis in Sappho's poem, in allowing for this triple shrine, while stressing the appeal to the powers of Hera, whom the Greeks associated especially with the life of women. She is the sister and wife of Zeus, divinity of marriage and of the sexual life of women. She at first rejected Zeus as a suitor, but when he landed on her lap as a cuckoo their marriage was consummated and their wedding night, passed on the island of Samos, lasted for 300 years. The goddess renewed her virginity every year by bathing in springs in Argos. Rituals connect her with the celebration of weddings and on works of art she is sometimes identified by her lifting of her veil, a sign of the bride's presentation to the groom. In addition to her association with the rites of marriage, and with childbirth, she is seen as the protector of cities and of specific communities. Although Argos, on the mainland of Greece, was a particular site of her cult, so too was the Aegean island of Samos, where a temple dedicated to Hera was erected as early as 800 BCE.

Sappho's fragment, although it refers to the three gods, appeals to Hera. In a later text, the *Palatine Anthology*, a poem instructs the women of Lesbos to come to the shining sanctuary of bull-faced Hera, and to dance there a beautiful dance for the goddess. The poet says that Sappho, with her golden lyre in her hands, will lead them in the dance. Even the muse Kalliope will contribute a sweet hymn. Given the fragmentary state of Sappho's hymn, we cannot know the nature of her appeal to the goddess Hera. It may concern a request associated with love, marriage or even childbirth. Or, since Hera was also associated with the triple shrine and the Homeric heroes' invocation of the three gods to enable their travel by sea back to the mainland of Greece, Sappho may here be offering a prayer for safety at sea and asking Hera to appear to her as a guarantor of her own or a loved one's voyage. In any case, we see here Sappho appealing not to Aphrodite, to Eros, to the Graces or the Muses, but rather to one of the great female divinities of this polytheistic world. Sappho, like the other inhabitants of antiquity until the rise of the monotheisms, not until the first century CE, at least 600 years after her lifetime, believed in and worshipped and honoured and supplicated many gods.

An educated woman, graced by the Muses, imbued with the knowledge of Homer and the narratives of the heroic age, Sappho was according to all reports an aristocrat, a member of the privileged elite of her society. Unlike many women of this and later periods of Greek antiquity, she was learned. Her role as a member of the aristocracy, daughter of the town of Eressos, inhabitant of the principal city of Lesbos, Mytilene, may have led her into the politics of the day. While she does not herself address the controversies of political regimes in the fragments we have, unless there are hidden meanings in the naming of particular objects of desire or scorn, later sources report that she was entangled in the conflicts of the sixth century BCE which, on Lesbos as elsewhere, involved struggles among aristocratic groups and confrontations with what the Greeks called 'tyrants'. The word *tyrannos*, 'tyrant', although it came later to be associated with practices we would designate as tyrannical, meant in the archaic period of Greece, Sappho's time, a monarch who had usurped power. Sometimes these figures emerged from aristocratic circles, allied themselves with the poor, with labouring people who would later have the rights of citizens, and broke the grip of the aristocracy on political and legal power. Such was the case in Athens, where the 'tyrant' Peisistratos, who seized power in the later sixth century BCE, paved the way for democracy by undermining the dominance of Athenian aristocrats.

Most city-states, as they began to grow, emerging from a time of disorganisation and of small populations mostly settled in tiny communities, found themselves with insufficient land and resources to support larger groups of people. Some sent out colonists, to found new city-states on the edges of the Mediterranean. In many there were conflicts among kings and aristocratic groups, between rival aristocratic families, and between the poor and the rich, who themselves were often the aristocrats, claiming rights to land that they traced back to their descent from heroes and even gods. Lesbos, and especially its principal city-state, Mytilene, was no exception. We find the traces of class conflict in the historical accounts of later writers and in the poetry of the archaic period. In several of the poems of Alkaios there are references to struggles among aristocratic groups and to the illegitimate seizure of power by individuals, called 'tyrants'. In his fragment 70, Alkaios refers to banqueting, but then alludes to a struggle between Myrsilos and Pittakos. He sang: 'let him, a relative by marriage of the sons of Atreus, gobble up the city as he once did in company with Myrsilos, until the god Ares call us to arms.' Ares, god of war, has sown conflict in the city, brought ruin to it and given fame and glory to Pittakos. A member of the house of Penthilidai, who at one time ruled over Mytilene, Pittakos and his family claimed to have descended from Penthilos, the son of Orestes, who was himself grandson of Atreus and therefore related to the great heroes of the Trojan war, Agamemnon and Menelaos. It may be that in the case of the sovereignty of Mytilene, Pittakos and Myrsilos ruled together over the city, but then fell out and took allies with them, in a rivalry that divided the aristocrats of the city.

Many of Alkaios' poems refer to a troubled city; fragment 6 shows a ship, like the city, tossed by waves, identified by a later commentary as troubles brought by tyrants. In his fragment 208, Alkaios uses the word *stasis*, 'civil strife', which also refers to the direction of the winds as a ship rolls, distressed in a great storm, identified by a later, ancient writer on allegory as a reference to the tyrannical conspiracy of Myrsilos. Fragment 60a, 'to the house of Hades', according to a later commentator curses the spear-carriers, the bodyguard of the tyrant. Many other fragments allude negatively, in a broken, almost indecipherable fashion now, to the tyrants. Fragment 298 seems to suggest that, like Ajax of Locris, Pittakos should have been stoned to death for violence to the gods and crimes against the Mytileneans. In another poem, preserved in the text of Athenaeus, Alkaios describes an armoury filled with what may be archaic weapons, bronze helmets, greaves to protect the shins, body armour of linen. He also refers to his own exile, said to be a consequence of his resistance to the tyranny of Pittakos over Mytilene. An earlier tyrant, Melankhros, may have been overthrown by this very Pittakos, in league with Alkaios' brothers. But then the tyrant Myrsilos assumed power. Alkaios appears to have been exiled several times, involved in conspiracies against both Myrsilos and Pittakos. The philosopher Aristotle cites a fragment of Alkaios, number 348, which complains that the Mytileneans elected Pittakos as tyrant, to handle the city's exiles, Pittakos whom he contemptuously calls *kakopatridan*, 'having a low-born father'. If he was exiled from Mytilene, Alkaios seems to have spent these periods on the island of Lesbos, in other cities, in Pyrrha, near the sanctuary of Hera, and elsewhere. In fragment 129, in which he mentions the great sanctuary of the three gods, among them Dionysos, eater of raw flesh, he again accuses 'Pot-belly', that is, Pittakos, and in fragment 130b says that he is living the life of a rustic, yearning to participate once again in the life of the city. He is in exile, *pheugon*, 'fleeing', using the language Sappho turned to erotic purpose in her fragment 1. Alkaios is hiding among the wolves, yearning to be freed by the Olympian gods.

All this trouble, the unrest in the city of Mytilene, and its multiple rulers, replacing aristocratic rule, provides context for our understanding of Sappho. Although these matters do not interrupt the erotic, hymnal, celebratory surface of her songs, she inhabited the same world as Alkaios, and her choice to sing not about politics but about eros, women's lives, marriage and Hera emphatically draws a line between the world of men and that of women of her class, of the aristocracy. Yet there is some ancient evidence that Sappho herself suffered in the *stasis*, the civil conflict internal to the city of Mytilene. Sappho is mentioned on an ancient source, the Parian Marble, an inscription erected in the third century BCE on the island of Paros. Now broken in two, one piece still on Paros, the other in Oxford, it gives a chronology, a date list, of various events with reference to the archons, the ruling magistrates of Athens, and goes all the way back to the Amazons' attack on the city, attempting to retrieve their queen from its ruler Theseus, camping out on the hill of the war god Ares, the Areopagos. The Parian Marble says that during the archonship of the first Kritias, 'Sappho sailed from Mytilene to Sicily, *phugousa*', that is, again, 'fleeing', 'in exile'. If that date is accurate, based on other sources, we can establish Sappho's exile as between 605 and 590 BCE. The inscription also says that the 'Gamoroi', wealthy landowners, were in power at this time in the city of Syracuse on the island of Sicily. Colonists from the city of Corinth had founded Syracuse in the eighth century BCE, and it had become a prosperous city, ruled at first by this aristocratic government, which itself sent out colonies. Syracuse may have welcomed Sappho, the renowned poet, an aristocratic exile from tyranny. Centuries later the Roman orator Cicero referred to a statue that had been erected to Sappho, that had stood in the *prytanium*, the town hall of Syracuse, and that had been stolen by a rapacious Roman proconsul, Verres. Reportedly a work by the artist Silanion, the portrait was taken and only an epigram remained on the base; Cicero mocks his opponent for his ignorance of Greek in the epigram which can only condemn the thief. Cicero, prosecuting Verres for his many crimes, says: 'how much this stolen Sappho was missed can barely be expressed.' Cicero says that the statue representing Sappho, now lost, was perfect and elegant. A papyrus from Egypt from the late second or early third century CE, that is, possibly 900 years after her life, describes Sappho's appearance as contemptible, ugly, dark and short. Is this slander, grafted onto a disapproval of her reputation as a lover of women? We will never know.

III

Sappho in Ancient Greece and Rome

UNDERSTANDING SAPPHO RELIES NOT ONLY on the frustratingly fragmentary nature of the poetry that remains to us. There are many layers, many filters, interested editing, approval and condemnation that enable and obscure our view of her world. And if our understanding of Sappho herself, in her own life, on her island of Lesbos, in her exile in Sicily, depends to a great extent on the beauties of her poetry, we have more information about her from those who came after her in antiquity. These include the great 'father of history', Herodotos, the comic poets of ancient Athens, Plato the philosopher, later poets including those of the Hellenistic age, the time after the death of Alexander the Great, as well as the poets of ancient Rome. And we have many reports from encyclopedic writers of later antiquity, those who wrote biographies or reports on obscure words used by the poets of the archaic and classical periods of Greece, some of these 1,600 years after the time of Sappho. So, although some of these sources come relatively near in time to the archaic age, the seventh and sixth centuries BCE, of Sappho's lifetime, and their information may be comparatively reliable, others are very distant, further from Sappho than we are from them, in the case for example of the *Suda*, compiled in the tenth century CE, that is, only a thousand years ago.

This *Suda*, along with other details of Sappho's life, reports that Sappho had three brothers, Larikhos, Kharaxos and Eurugios. One of these brothers figures in her fragment 5, a prayer to Aphrodite and the Nereids to bring her brother back from wherever he has been:

> O Kypris and Nereids grant that unharmed
> my brother arrive back here to me.
> And whatever his heart wishes to happen,
>   grant that all this will happen.
>
> And however many times before he missed the mark, let it go,
> and let him become a delight to his loved ones,
> and a grief for his enemies. And may there never more be
>   anyone who is a misery to us.
>
> And may he then want his sister to partake in honor,
> but sore grief ...   ... before in sorrow ...

This poem, along with another recently restored fragment, to be discussed in Chapter 4, tells the story of a brother who has been a trouble to Sappho's family. She wishes that he will repent and become a joy to his dear ones, a pain to his enemies; this is a characteristic move on the part of the ancient Greeks, who saw such discrimination between friends and enemies as a crucial aspect of social life. It seems likely that the prayer seeks safe landing after a sea voyage, since the Nereids, daughters of Nereus, live with their father at the bottom of the sea and could watch over his return. The request made to 'the Kyprian', 'Kypris', that is, Aphrodite from Cyprus, suggests that the troubles of Sappho's brother may have something to do with eros, that the goddess herself has punished the brother for crimes of love.

Fragments 7 and 15 mention a woman called Dorikha; number 15, from a second-century CE papyrus, again addresses Kypris, and continues 'may she, Dorikha, not vaunt that he came a second time to a yearned-for eros'. The fifth-century BCE historian Herodotos, who came from Halikarnassos, a Greek city in Asia Minor, travelled west, read his work in Athens and settled in the Athenian outpost Thurii in southern Italy. In his great history of the Persian Wars of the fifth century, fought between several Persian emperors and the shakily united Greek states of the day, Herodotos offers anthropological observations on various peoples, including the Egyptians, and tells the prehistory of those Greeks who successfully fended off two Persian invasions of mainland Greece. He touches on the life of Sappho, as he gives a brief account of the adventures of Sappho's brother Kharaxos.

Herodotos tells us that there was, during the reign of the Egyptian Pharaoh Amasis, who reigned from 568 to 526 BCE, a woman named not Dorikha, but Rhodopis. The name means 'face of a rose', 'rose-faced'. A certain Xanthes of Samos had brought her to Egypt, apparently to practise her trade as a *hetaira*, that is, a geisha-like courtesan of the day. She must have been a slave, since the historian reports that Kharaxos, son of Skamandronymos and brother of the poet Sappho, freed her by means of a great deal of money. Furthermore, after freeing Rhodopis from slavery, Herodotos says that Kharaxos returned to the city of Mytilene, where his sister mocked him exceedingly. Further detail concerning Rhodopis comes from Athenaeus, who came himself from the port of Naukratis and was author of the *Deipnosophistai, Learned Banqueters* or *Scholars at Dinner*, a many-volumed work cited previously. He reports that Naukratis had many well-known *hetairai*. One was Dorikha; he says that the beautiful Sappho accused her in her poetry, on the grounds that she had stolen a great deal from her brother. Athenaeus acknowledges the confusion made by Herodotos between Dorikha and Rhodopis, and goes on to note that Rhodopis dedicated metal roasting spits at Delphi. He remarks also that the Hellenistic poet Posidippos, who lived in the third century BCE, wrote an epigram, a brief poem or inscription, on Dorikha, which invokes this woman, who of course might have been nicknamed Rhodopis, 'face like a rose', 'rosy-faced'. Posidippos' poem, in honour of Sappho, goes:

> Dorikha, your delicate bones slept the sleep of death
> the bands of your hair, your shawl, breathing out perfumes,
> with which, once upon a time, wrapping graceful Kharaxos
> skin to skin you clung to the early morning, the ivy drinking cups.
> But Sappho's sounding white pages, her dear song, still remain and will remain;
> enviable your name, which Naukratis in this way will keep watch over
> so long as a ship of the Nile goes on the salt seas.

Just as Homer gave the name of Akhilleus immortal life, so Sappho has immortalised the *hetaira* Dorikha. Though she and her lover are dead, and she lies wrapped in a shroud, some of the papyri on which Sappho's words are recorded survive and, indeed, ships still sail from the Nile, and we remember Dorikha.

The later geographer Strabo also mentions the tale of Dorikha/Rhodopis in his description of Egypt. He lists among the pyramids to be found near the city of Memphis one called 'of the *hetaira*', the courtesan, and says that it was constructed by her lovers. Other late authors confirm the status of Rhodopis, declaring that she was Thracian by birth, from the northern edge of the Mediterranean; they say that she slaved alongside the fabulist Aesop, for the Mytilenean Iadmon, and that Sappho's brother 'ransomed' her, that is, bought her, or bought her freedom. Strabo too says that she was the beloved of Sappho's brother, and he calls her Dorikha, as does Sappho, although he notes that others name her Rhodopis. He adds that this brother of the poet brought Lesbian wine to Naukratis in Egypt. Naukratis was a trading post, an *emporion*, 'emporium', founded by various cities of the Greek eastern Mediterranean acting together, including Mytilene. It received concessions from the pharaoh Amasis but seems to have pre-dated his reign. Before the foundation of the great city of Alexandria by Alexander the Great in the fourth century BCE, Naukratis was the main centre of commercial and cultural exchange between the Greeks and the Egyptians. So her brother's contact with Africa, her own attention to Lydia and especially to Sardis, and the reported exile in Sicily all extend the range of Sappho's world to include much of the Mediterranean, south, east and west. We may understand her to be the poet of Mytilene, of Lesbos, but her life and her connections touch on much of the world known to the Greeks in her day.

Strangely enough, one ancient source, Aelian, says there were two Sapphos on Lesbos: the poet and another, a *hetaira* herself. There are other reports concerning Sappho's erotic life, besides the naming of her husband as Mr Prick from the island of Man. She was said to have been the object of sexual advances on the part of her contemporary Alkaios, and to have refused him. The scene between them was represented in vase painting. Allegedly, Alkaios sang of his love for her, annoying another suitor, the poet Anakreon, who wrote: 'Eros with his golden hair, throwing his bright, purple ball at me, calls me out to play with an ornately-sandalled girl ...' This is the Lesbian maiden who rejects him because he has white hair and goes gaping after another girl. And although Anakreon actually lived somewhat later than Sappho, since he was born about 570 BCE, allegedly Sappho wrote a poem back to him, complimenting him and saying that the Muse uttered his poem, from the land of beautiful women.

There were other female poets, probably writing later than Sappho herself, of whose work we have only the most meagre of fragments. Plutarch mentions Myrtis, a lyric poet from Boeotia, north of Attica, who was born in the late sixth century BCE. The poet Korinna, whose dates have been contested, was said by some to be a contemporary of Sappho; others said she was a student of Myrtis, from Thebes or the town of Tanagra. She was called a rival of Pindar, poet of the first half of the fifth century BCE, whom she is said to have defeated in poetic contests, although other evidence points to a life in the late third or even first century BCE. She wrote choral, narrative poems, so far as we can ascertain from the fragments that survive, songs that may have been performed by groups of girls and that often reflect the local concerns of Boeotia, site of the important city of Thebes, home of Oidipous in the heroic past. One concerns a confrontation between Helicon and Kithaeron, two mountains competing in a singing contest. Another relates that Terpsichore, one of the Muses, summons the singer to recount beautiful stories for the 'white-robed women of Tanagra'. She was reported to have written a narrative poem, 'Seven against Thebes', subject in the fifth century BCE of a tragedy by Aeschylus. The legend describes the siege of Thebes by seven heroes led by the son of Oidipous, Polyneikes. The fragments of Korinna reveal the legacy of Homer, a narrative, heroic bent, without the focus on eros that we find in the lyric poets, among them her predecessor Sappho.

Plutarch tells a story of the poet Telesilla, who seems to have lived in the fifth century BCE; like many other features of ancient biographies, this legend may have more to do with invention based on misunderstood information than with fact. Kleomenes, the king of Sparta, attacked Argos, another city in the Peloponnesos, and Telesilla was said to have urged the Argive women to fight. After many men were killed, the women armed themselves and stood on the ramparts of their city; the Spartans, astonished, were fended off after losing many of their troops. Not only a warrior, saviour of her city, Telesilla was said to be an even greater poet than fighter. Few lines of her verse survive; some say that her words inspired warriors as the poets Tyrtaios roused the Spartans and Alkaios the Lesbians. Another woman poet, Kharixena, is known, but we have nothing of her writing; later writers call her old-fashioned, and stupid for it, but she was said to compose erotic songs. Athenaeus names Praxilla, of Sicyon near Corinth, but we know little about her except that she was said to have composed drinking songs. A commentator cites her: 'Under every stone there is a scorpion; my friend, watch out!' Another intriguing fragment, context unknown, by Praxilla, runs: 'O you, beautifully looking in through the window, maiden ... , beneath a bride'. The beginning words of this fragment were found inscribed on a vase dated to about 450 BCE.

Erinna, a poet of the fourth century BCE, was said by some to have been born on Lesbos; she wrote a poem about weaving and spinning, 'The Distaff', and a fragment survives lamenting a friend, Baucis, who died young. An anonymous work of the *Palatine Anthology* asserts that just as Sappho's lyrics are better than Erinna's, by so much do Erinna's hexameters, that is, epic metres, surpass Sappho's. The poet Nossis, who peaked, 'flourished', that is, around 300 BCE, in the southern Italian town of Locri Epizephyrii, that is Locri lying towards the west, towards the west wind, wrote epigrams meant for inscriptions on works of art; she compared herself to Sappho and also wrote poetry on love and desire. In one fragment she addresses a traveller and asks that if the stranger is sailing to Mytilene, place of the lovely dances, in order to catch fire from Sappho's blossoming graces, she should say that the voice in the poem, a friend to Sappho and the Muses, comes from the land of Locri. And that her name is Nossis. One of Nossis' fragments speaks to the goddess Hera and asks her to accept an offering. Another asks Artemis to rescue a woman named Alketis from labour pains. An epigram speaks as if addressing a passer-by from a tomb and says that the passer-by, after laughing and leaving a friendly word, should know that the person depicted is Rhinthon, from Syracuse, 'a little nightingale of the Muses'. Another woman writer, whose work is found in the *Palatine Anthology*, Anyte, came from Arcadia in the Peloponnesos and lived in the later fourth century BCE. She wrote epigrams, like other poets discussed here, often epitaphs, poems technically written for gravestones but probably performed in recitations. She composed poems that describe works of art, epitaphs for the tombs of young women and verses on the deaths of animals. She also sang about the landscape of rural people, the pleasures of cold springs, sightings of the goat god Pan, perhaps concerning Arcadia, which becomes in literary tradition the hallowed site of this god and of pastoral poetry. In the development of this genre, which extends beyond Anyte to the Hellenistic poet Theokritos, to Virgil, and into the Renaissance, to Philip Sidney's sixteenth-century work *The Countess of Pembroke's Arcadia*, and further, to some of the greatest poems of John Milton, poets and shepherds converse, engage in singing contests of great sophistication and also appear in works of visual art. The great seventeenth-century French painter Nicolas Poussin, who painted and died in Rome, portrayed shepherds around a tomb with the legend *Et in Arcadia ego*: 'I [that is, Death] am [here, even] in Arcadia.' Anyte even writes an epitaph for a slave, in a move highly unusual for an ancient Greek poet: 'This Manes lived as a slave, but dead, he can now be as powerful as Darius the Great.' That is, the man with a typical slave name has died, and in the land of the dead, he will be just as powerful as the dead Persian emperor. We have the names, and only the tiniest of fragments of other women poets, Moiro, Hedyla, Melinno, each of them, nonetheless, in the genealogy of Sappho.

The *Suda* gives a brief narrative, possibly about 'the other' Sappho, that was to have a long life and that eventually, in modernity, turns Sappho into a tragic heterosexual, to the relief of some fanciers of her poetry. The listing says: 'this Sappho, on account of her love for the Mytilenean Phaon, threw herself from the cliff of Leukates and drowned.' Strabo the geographer has told this tale before, when describing Leukas; he says that Sappho, hunting the arrogant Phaon, pitched herself through tormenting desire from that far-visible cliff, on an island near Odysseus' island of Ithaka, or from that island itself, according to some. In the *Odyssey* the suitors of Penelope, having been killed by the hero and his allies, pass the stream of Ocean and 'the white rock', led by Hermes, the god who takes the dead into the underworld. Strabo is citing Menander, the fourth-century BCE comedy writer, who, in the play *Leukadia*, now lost, seems to have referred to this story. The story of Sappho's frustrated love for Phaon and her suicide off the 'white rock', the promontory of Leukates, may have been an invention of the comic poets, mocking her and creating this unlikely, counterfactual lust, for laughs, in contrast to her evident desire for girls and women. The island of Leukas, or Lefkada, is far from Lesbos, off the western coast of Greece; its name, from the adjective *leukos*, 'light/bright/white', comes from the cliffs of white limestone along its western coast. According to Strabo, during an annual ritual at the festival dedicated to the god Apollo, in a sort of scapegoat or *pharmakos* rite, a criminal was thrown from the top, 'to avert evil'. Birds and wings were attached to him, to break his fall. If he survived, people waiting below in fishing boats pulled him from the sea and took him beyond the borders of the Leucadians. The poet Anakreon also sings of diving off 'the white rock', drunk on eros.

Phaon, according to some, is another name for Adonis, the lover of Aphrodite who died young and was mourned in the rituals of the Adoneia, for which Sappho seems to have composed songs of lamentation; when Aphrodite confessed her love for the son of Kinyras, ancient readers may have understood Sappho herself to be speaking of her desire for Phaon. Phaon was said to ferry passengers across a strait of the sea; he accepted a fare only from the rich. When Aphrodite appeared to him disguised as an old woman, he carried her across and demanded no payment. In exchange she transformed what had been an old man and gave him beauty and youth, hiding him among lettuces as she did Adonis, and because of these attributes the poet Sappho fell in love with him. Another peculiar detail, another version of his powers, comes from the first-century CE Roman author Pliny, who in his *Natural History* alleges that a plant called 'sea-holly' takes the shape of either male or female genitals; when a man finds it, and finds the male shape, he becomes sexually desirable. This made Sappho fall in love with Phaon, in this version of the tale said to be from Lesbos.

A fascinating interpretation of this episode from the legends concerning Sappho comes from the classicist Gregory Nagy (in a chapter in Ellen Green's *Reading Sappho*, and elsewhere), who sees very ancient roots in the story of the poet in love with a ferryman, as Phaon came to be known, and her throwing herself from the 'white rock'. It seems that the leap off the rock had long been a cure for love; Zeus sat on the rock to relieve himself of his desire for Hera. Aphrodite herself had jumped from the white rock for love of Adonis. Tracing a web, a network of associations, Nagy describes 'the white rock' as the boundary between consciousness and unconsciousness, wakefulness and sleep, life and death. Looking to parallels with the ancient Sanskrit *Rig Veda*, a collection of hymns to the gods, and following other vestiges in Greek myth, Nagy sees a pattern of disappearance in the rise of the morning star and the setting of the evening star, and Aphrodite as embodying these astral recurrences, pursuing the sun. The beautiful Phaon may be connected to Phaethon, son of the sun, the youth who once drove Helios' chariot, carrying the sun across the day's sky until he was unable to control the horses, was killed by his father with a thunderbolt and fell into the river Eridanos. The leap of the lover Aphrodite, an analogue of the goddess of dawn and sunset, recovers the sun, or Phaon, and also restores her youth and beauty.

> From Menander fragment 258 K., we infer that Sappho spoke of herself as diving from the White Rock, crazed with love for Phaon. The implications of this image are cosmic. The 'I' of Sappho's poetry is vicariously projecting her identity into the goddess Aphrodite, who loves the native Lesbian hypostasis of the Sun-God himself. By diving from the White Rock, the 'I' of Sappho does what Aphrodite does in the form of Evening Star, diving after the sunken Sun in order to

retrieve him, another morning, in the form of Morning Star. If we imagine her pursuing the Sun the night before, she will be pursued in turn the morning after.

(Nagy, in *Reading Sappho*, p. 55)

Plunging off the white rocks is linked to the sun and its preservation, as it rises each morning after disappearing every evening. And if Sappho identifies, pursuing and then fleeing in the first of her poems, with Aphrodite, sees herself in the goddess, her *summakhos*, then Sappho's association with the leap off the white rocks may speak to her desire for preservation, restoration, the return of youth to an ageing mortal body, a theme we will consider in Chapter 4.

Giving Sappho many male lovers seems to have been one of the great jokes of the Athenian comic writers of the classical age. After the archaic period, the time of tyrants and great civil strife, of the dominance of aristocrats in many cities, the city of Athens worked its way slowly but surely towards democracy, that is, rule by the *demos*, 'the people'. The understanding of *demos*, people, varies; sometimes it refers to all the citizens, all those who can trace their family roots back into the city's past, all those men formally accepted into the institutions that make up the *polis*, the 'city-state'. At other times, especially in the works of those who preferred aristocratic or oligarchic rule, government by the 'best', the nobility, or by the 'few', the rich, it refers to the poor, the mob, those citizens pressing always for more equality in the city's governance. In the case of Athens, the so-called radical democracy of the fifth century BCE, that is, at least a hundred years after the time of Sappho, was an unprecedented experiment in citizen self-rule. And in the context of Persian invasion and defeat, internal conflict, war with the Spartans and their allies, the overthrowing of democracy and its restoration, the Athenians, wealthy and bent on domination of their part of the world, made drama, both tragedy and comedy, part of their political existence. The commitment to drama was remarkable, part of a form of ritual, honouring the god Dionysos, god of wine and theatre, but also a form of political debate. Tragedy often addressed such questions as guilt and shame, human versus immortal responsibility for terrible events, the relations between the gods and men, gender and power, slavery and war. Tragedy, after its earliest performances, which did, for example, show the court of the defeated Persians, does not refer directly to the events of the audience's present, nor to persons of that present, even though the political and social struggles of the city took shape on the tragic stage through the presentation of gods and heroes from the past.

Comedy, on the other hand, used invented plots, and frequently addressed and ridiculed prominent figures in the city, and probably in the audience of the performances as well. As was tragedy, comedy was a part of the ritual celebration of the god Dionysos, patron of the vineyards and wine made in Attica, the territory surrounding the city of Athens. It may have evolved from processions led in honour of the god, with participants carrying phalluses, representations of erect penises, as signs of the fertility requested and given by the god to the city. The actors wore costumes with padded buttocks and penises and engaged in a great deal of obscene banter, as noted, sometimes directed to members of the audience. And, just as in tragedy, female characters on the comic stage were played by male actors, boys and men, some of whom became famous for their transvestite skills. Only the fifth- and early fourth-century BCE comic plays of Aristophanes and Menander survive in their entirety. Aristophanes, the great genius of 'Old Comedy', composed fabulous plots obliquely implicating the politics of his day. *Lysistrata*, for example, produced in 411 BCE, towards the end of the Peloponnesian War between the Spartans and their allies on one side and the Athenians and theirs on the other, depicts a sex strike led by an Athenian priestess and involving women from the opposing sides. They unite to end the war, refusing to have sex with their husbands until peace is declared. There is much obscenity and ridicule, pointing fingers at prominent Athenians in the audience, and a riotous conclusion. The actors, of course, were all boys and men. The comic force of the play derives in part from the impossibility of such events.

Other plays are named after their choruses, which were a constant feature of both tragedy and comedy: the *Wasps* mocks the Athenian jury system; the *Birds* describes the creation by birds of a utopian city in the clouds; and the *Clouds* ridicules Socrates and may have contributed to popular opinion and the death penalty imposed on him in 399 BCE. The later comic writer Menander, who wrote in the fourth-century BCE, the principal figure in 'New Comedy', composed plots centred on contemporary Athens or its surrounding territory, Attica, and concerned with domestic matters, a young man and woman, for example, separated by some obstacle, fate or an irascible father. Slaves, *hetairai* or courtesans, and other non-elite characters figure prominently in his works. We have most of one surviving play, *Dyskolos*, *The Grouch*, which features a misanthropic father and a marriage plot. Menander's plots had a great influence on Roman comedy, and subsequently on the comedies of the Renaissance, on Shakespeare, among others.

Neither Aristophanes nor Menander, however, wrote anything resembling a play about a female poet of the archaic age. So how do we understand Sappho's appearance on the comic stage of Athens, in several comedies, according to later sources? Comic writers whose works we have only in sorely fragmentary form did apparently write comedies based on myths, and on contemporary political figures. Athenaeus reports that the comic poet Diphilos (fourth century BCE) wrote a play called *Sappho*, in which he portrayed both Arkhilokhos and Hipponax, men, as lovers of Sappho. Athenaeus also quotes the play, with a mere two lines, someone offering a cup to Arkhilokhos, in honour of the Saviour Zeus and the god of good fortune. And Athenaeus, in an extended section on riddles in his huge work, also says that the character 'Sappho', in Antiphanes' comedy, sets riddles for solution. He cites one at length, in verse:

> Sappho says: There is a female being which guards its offspring safely under its breast; these, although voiceless, raise a loud-sounding shout both over the sea's swell and over all the land, to whomever of mortals they wish; and it's possible even for those not present to hear; but their sense of hearing is dull.

Another character in the play proposes that the answer to the riddle is the *polis*, the 'city-state', whose offspring are the speakers, who by their screaming drag profits from across the sea, from Asia and from Thrace. The 'people', *demos*, sit by them while they consume and revile one another, hearing and seeing nothing. He offers, then, a critique of the politics of the city. 'Sappho' replies that this is the wrong answer: 'how could a speaker, a politician, a rhetorician, be voiceless?' He could be barred from the assembly for proposing too many unconstitutional measures. But this Sappho solves the riddle herself:

> The feminine being is a written message, a letter, an epistle; the offspring are the letters, *grammata*, which it carries about. These, being voiceless, talk to whomever they wish to when far away; but if another person happens to stand near as it is read, he will not hear.

Sappho has become a literate, witty woman of letters, baffling her interlocutors with enigmatic play. Unfortunately, this is all we hear about this tantalising work; the play is lost. But there were other comedies called *Sappho*, and we have just a few lines from each, by Timokles and Ephippos, single words from Ameipsias and Amphis. Some other plays have titles preserved that may indicate Sapphic subject matter, including two called *Phaon*, one by 'Plato Komikos', a writer about whom little is known except that this play was probably produced in 391 BCE, and another by Antiphanes, the author of the riddling Sappho. There also appear to have been plays, now lost, called *The Leucadian*, which may also refer to Phaon, and perhaps, his adventure with Sappho. What do we make of the appearance of Sappho in comedy, how does it help us understand who she was, or how ancient people, just two or three centuries after her death, saw her? Difficult to know.

The vase painters of the classical Greek period represented Sappho in works of art, and we still have at least four vases on which Sappho has been definitively identified, although there is speculation about her image on some others, since a woman dancing, carrying a musical instrument, may be Sappho or another anonymous woman poet, singer, dancer. But several of the vases bear labels, with Sappho's name painted on or incised in the clay of the ceramic vase. A sixth-century BCE vase shows her holding a lyre; this vase has been found to depict an ugly Sappho, like the one described in some later sources, although others argue that the portrait is consistent with other such images of the period. A vase that shows a lyre-playing woman on one side, another, cloaked woman on the other, may represent a situation like that depicted in Sappho's first fragment, where she prays to Aphrodite to make the girl who flees her into her pursuer. Another vase from the fifth century BCE shows a beautiful Sappho, carrying her musical instrument, and a male figure, also a musician, with a different instrument, labelled Alkaios. They seem to be engaged in amicable conversation, although a tradition grew up, referred to earlier, that Alkaios had made sexual advances towards Sappho, perhaps in a poem, calling her 'violet-haired, holy, sweetly-smiling', and that she nonetheless had rejected him, as she did other poetic male suitors. A *hydria*, a water jug, from the 440s BCE, appears to shows Sappho reading from a scroll. It bears the word *theoi*, 'gods', and then, 'I begin with early morning words …' Then, perhaps, a commentary: *pteroeta epea*, 'winged words'. One scholar argued that these were the first words of the first poem of the first book of Sappho's works.

The earliest Greek philosophers, or proto-philosophers, took on such weighty questions as the nature of the substance of the cosmos, whether infinite or finite. Some wrote in verse; some proposed various material origins – water, fire, for example – as the beginning of the things of the world. Other Presocratics, as they came to be known much later, were concerned with mathematics and the soul, as was Pythagoras. Some thought the material world to be made up of tiny, indestructible particles, or atoms. The 'sophists', wandering teachers of rhetoric, questioned the received ideas of the classical world and taught the sons of the newly wealthy to participate in the political debates of their cities. These thinkers were all relegated to an early stage of philosophy by later scholars, who regarded philosophy itself to have begun as a practice with the 'Socratics', that is, the Athenians Socrates, his disciple Plato and his student Aristotle. Socrates himself left no writing behind, only the memory of his life as recorded by others. The most significant vestiges of his life can be read in the dialogues of Plato, some of which feature a character named 'Socrates' in conversation with various others. Sappho, who was by this time, in the fourth century BCE, a renowned poet of 200 years earlier, appears not as a character, but as a point of reference, as the beautiful author of beautiful and moving lyric poetry. The *Palatine Anthology*, a collection of poems recorded by scribes in the tenth century CE but including poems going back to the seventh century BCE, contains this, attributed to Plato himself: 'nine are the Muses, some say; how carelessly; see there – Sappho from Lesbos is the tenth.'

Plato invokes Sappho directly, in the dialogue called *Phaedrus*, named after Socrates' partner in conversation in this great work on love and writing. Socrates and the young Phaidros/Phaedrus go for a walk in the country. Phaidros reads to him a work he admires, on love, by the eloquent Lysias, arguing for the boy's or man's giving of (sexual) favours to another man who pursues him but does not love him. Socrates finds the speech, even as rhetoric, to be unsatisfactory, and says that he has heard something better from the wise men and women of the past who have written on this theme. 'I'm positive I have heard better, from the beautiful Sappho, perhaps, or wise Anakreon, or a prose writer.' He feels something welling up in his breast that has been poured into him from some source; and, covering his head, summoning the Muses, he delivers a speech arguing the same point as Lysias', for the non-lover's superiority as a lover. But then, before he and Phaidros can leave the spot, sacred to the nymphs, he is warned by his 'daimon', his divine sign, which always stops him when he is about to go wrong. He has offended Eros, who is a god. Like Stesikhoros, who offended Helen, he must recant.

Then Socrates the character delivers a magnificent oration in praise of the true lover, inspired by the gods Aphrodite and Eros. Of the four kinds of divine madness, one comes from the Muses, seizes 'a tender, virginal soul', and leads it to the composition of lyric poetry (like Sappho's). And eros, sent by the gods, is a great gift, bringing bliss. The lover sees his beloved and is taken by divine erotic madness. The immortal soul once glimpsed beauty; the sight of the lover awakens the memory of that true beauty, and the language Plato uses here summons the memory of Sappho's lines, in fragment 31, on the sight of her beloved, as her heart trembles, she is rendered speechless, her tongue snaps, fire runs beneath her skin, she cannot see, her ears buzz, sweat pours from her, she trembles, greener than grass, and feels herself to be near death. Socrates describes the lover, taken by the divine madness of eros, as he looks on his beloved. Sight is the most acute of our senses, he says, and it can perceive beauty. His description of the lover's gaze at the beloved is deeply influenced by Sappho's poem, which calls the man sitting by her beloved 'equal to the gods', *isos theoisin*. Plato says that the lover, seeing a godlike, *theoeides*, face, first shivers. Then awe comes over him, and if he weren't to be considered mad, he would sacrifice to his beloved, as to a divine statue, or a god. He shivers, and then, in response, sweating and a strange heat take him. The trembling, the fire, the overpowering physical reaction to the sight of the beloved, all these look back to Sappho and her description in fragment 31. Plato goes on, building on this set of symptoms, to describe further warming of the lover, as the flowing of beauty into his eyes enters him and the dormant feathers of the soul soften and grow, as the soul throbs with heat and gushes forth, and, while it gazes upon the beauty of the boy, particles, *mere*, flow to it, resulting in desire, *himeros*. This process produces both pleasure and pain, the joy of the gaze, the pain of longing, *pothos*. These themes too recall many of Sappho's poems, saturated as they are with yearning for an absent beloved.

All this part of the dialogue can be read in light of Plato's summoning of Sappho to Socrates' side. In Plato's view, however, the true lover, with his immortal soul, recognises human beauty as he gazes upon his lover. If his experience with the eternal beauty is fresh in him, he can resist physical gratification of his desire and move towards a recognition of that eternal, imperishable beauty that resides beyond human, material experience. Sappho's fragment 16, which defines the most beautiful thing on the black earth as 'whatever one loves', names an individual, Anaktoria. Both using Sappho's language and repudiating her choice at the same time, Plato leaves the domain of human eros to describe a metaphysical, transcendent, philosophical love, in which individual human beings must go beyond physical, material reality, to try to return to a gaze at an eternal, perfect origin. He compares the reasoning part of the soul to a chariot whose charioteer must master two horses, one modest, one wild and unruly. The bad horse must be trained through violent means, must be reined in, his tongue and jaws bleeding from the bit, so that the lovers resist physical enjoyment even as they lie together, and their winged, feathered souls after death will go forward on their upward journey, back to the sight of eternal beauty and good. Sappho, offering an entirely different understanding of human love, might have given rein to the bad horse.

Sappho, for Plato, was the tenth Muse, a poet like a god. Khamaileon wrote a treatise, 'On Sappho', in the fourth century BCE. After the classical period, the time of Athenian drama, tragedy and comedy, as well as the Socratic philosophers, her fame persisted. Sometimes later writers honoured her as another muse; Aelian (second and third century CE) said of Solon, the sixth-century BCE lawgiver of Athens, that when his nephew sang a poem of Sappho with the wine, Solon asked the boy to teach it to him and he said it was so he could learn it, and die. We know that the songs of Sappho were long performed at symposia, drinking parties. The fourth-century BCE Epikrates boasts that he has thoroughly learned the love songs of Sappho, along with those of other poets. The father of Alexander the Great, Philip II of Macedon, conquered mainland Greece in the fourth century BCE, not long after the death of Plato. He recruited Plato's student, Aristotle, to tutor his son Alexander. Aristotle was the great thinker who followed his teacher but also entered into a vast enterprise encompassing the histories of philosophy and politics, works on logic and biology, metaphysics and ethics, poetry and rhetoric, in a dazzling series of works. Although he honoured Plato, and the gods of the Greeks, he did not share all of his views. Yet, citing Sappho in his treatise on rhetoric, as useful in argument based on precedents, he said: 'Sappho says that dying is an evil; for the gods have made this judgement, for otherwise they would die.' On induction in argument, he cited a rhetorician who proved that all men honour the wise, by listing various unlikely examples of such honour; the Mytileneans honoured Sappho even though she was a woman.

Alexander inherited his father's kingdom and went on to conquer vast territories and populations, including the whole of the Persian Empire, Egypt and lands far to the east. In 331 BCE he founded the city of Alexandria, which replaced the port of Naukratis as the principal Greek city in Egypt. Alexander established many other Alexandrias as he marched across western Asia, eventually reaching the Hyphasis river, in what is now north-western

India, where his armies mutinied and he was forced to turn back. After a difficult journey, he died in Babylon in 323 BCE. His generals fought over the territories he had barely mastered; the Macedonian general Ptolemy won Egypt and the Egyptian Alexandria. He and his heirs sought to consolidate their reign by adopting some indigenous Egyptian practices, such as brother–sister marriage, fusing Greek and Egyptian gods and receiving in Alexandria the peoples of the vicinity. The second Ptolemy built a great Mouseion, dedicated to the Muses, the ancestor of our museums, and a huge library. Among those who moved to the city, attracted by its wealth and support for Greek culture, were poets from throughout the Greek world. Students and scholars, including Jews from Judaea, began to practise forms of criticism, trying to sort out original texts from later encrustations, translating ancient works, attempting to understand the meaning of words no longer in use. Learned Jews were brought from Jerusalem to translate into Greek the Torah, the Pentateuch of the ancient Israelites. And some of the finest literary works of this period, called the 'Hellenistic', show reverence for the archaic lyric poet Sappho of 400 years earlier. Many of the fragments we still have, from the nine books of Sappho's verse, come from papyrus found in Egypt, copies made by students and scholars that were eventually discarded in the sands and not recovered until the modern period, some still being discovered today in collections in libraries in Europe that preserve these fragments.

Among the poetic tributes to Sappho are epigrams ascribed to her found in the *Palatine Anthology*, the manuscript discovered in 1606 CE in Heidelberg, in Germany. Other pages were sent to Paris and remain there. It contains three poems, 'epigrams' perhaps once inscribed on gravestones, attributed to Sappho but probably not hers, written rather by poets of the Hellenistic age. The epigram has a fascinating history; the gravestone 'spoke', as if it had a voice, often the voice of the dead person or persons to whom the stone, the stele, was dedicated. Herodotos records an epigram written on the gravestone commemorating the warriors of the battle of Thermopylae in northern Greece, killed by the Persians as they tried to block the invading army as it passed into Greece. This inscription by the poet Simonides, addressed to any passer-by, read: 'Stranger, announce to the Spartans that we lie here, obedient to their words.' Ancient readers often read aloud; they would thus sound out the words, ventriloquising the voices of the deceased.

One of the epigrams allegedly by Sappho herself was inscribed on the tomb of a fisherman, Pelagon, whose father Meniskos speaks, saying that he placed there his son's creel and his oar, as a remembrance of his miserable life. Another, which seems most Sapphic in its themes, referring to the companions of a lost friend, says: 'These are the ashes of Timas; Persephone received her, dying before her wedding, into her dark chamber. When she died, all her age-mates shaved from their heads their lovely hair, with newly whetted iron.' A third epigram, unlike these, seems to have been written to adorn a statue, which itself addresses the reader:

> Children, voiceless as I am, I speak back if anyone asks, since I have an untiring voice set down before my feet. To Aithopia, daughter of Leto, Arista the daughter of Hermoklides, son of Saunaiadas, dedicated me. She is your priestess, mistress of women; take joy in her, gladly praise our family.

Like the voiceless letter of the comic Sappho, and the immortal daughters of Dioskorides' Sappho, also from the *Palatine Anthology*, the words inscribed by a respectful imitator of the archaic poet preserve her, as well as Aithopia and Arista, in memory. In the *Anakreontea*, poems written in the spirit of the earlier poet Anakreon, in the Hellenistic, perhaps in the Roman or even Byzantine, Christian, era, and also found in the *Palatine Anthology*, Sappho is called 'sweet singing'.

The Hellenistic poets were self-consciously literate and literary, unlike the singers who composed, orally, the *Iliad* and the *Odyssey*. They had access to much more of the classical Greek tradition than we do now; the famous library of Alexandria contained collections of the works of the great authors of the past, as many as half a million scrolls, estimated as equivalent to a library of 100,000 'books' today; there was another library at Pergamon in Asia Minor. The Alexandria library's collections were lost over centuries; Julius Caesar, when in Egypt in 48 BCE, allegedly set fire to the Mouseion in which the scrolls were held, and later fires continued the destruction of its collections. But in the Hellenistic period, before Roman involvement in the governance of Egypt, under the Ptolemies, including Cleopatra, scholarship flourished.

The Hellenistic epic poet Apollonios Rhodios, a learned man from Alexandria or Naukratis, was a librarian and tutor in third-century BCE Alexandria. In addition to labouring in the great library, Apollonios Rhodios wrote a long saga that was indebted not only to his epic predecessors but also to Greek tragedy, especially the poet Euripides, and even before that, to the lyric poets, including Sappho. His great poem the *Argonautica* tells the story of the voyage of the Argonauts, sailors on the *Argo*, the first ship ever built, captained by the hero Jason. They sail from Iolkos in northern Greece to the far eastern coast of the Black Sea to recover the golden fleece, the fleece of a ram who had carried Phrixos to the kingdom of the sun, ruled by King Aeetes, father of Medea, herself a granddaughter of the sun, Helios. Set various ordeals by the king, Jason wins the heart of Medea, who helps him plough a field with bulls that breathe fire, sow it with the teeth of a dragon and kill the armed warriors who rise up from the ground. Medea helps him seize the fleece, which was guarded by a monstrous dragon.

Apollonios' description of Medea in love owes a debt not only to Euripides' fifth-century BCE tragedies of lovelorn women, *Phaidra* and *Medea*, but also to Sappho's account in fragment 31 of her physical disintegration at the sight of her lover. In Book 3 of the *Argonautica*, Apollonios portrays Eros delivering the arrow of desire to Medea. She is rendered speechless, and the arrow burns in her heart like a flame, panting in its anguish. She loses memory of everything else, and her soul begins to melt with the sweet pain of desire. The colour of her cheeks runs from pale to crimson. Later, she gazes at the hero as her heart smoulders with pain. And in a subsequent scene, her spirit flutters for joy, her skin flushes and a mist overtakes her as she melts in desire. Unable to sleep, again she feels the physical symptoms of a smouldering flesh, a throbbing heart, a quivering in her breast. When Jason comes to her, once again her heart falls from her breast, her eyes are misted over and she blushes. She cannot move. Again and again, Apollonios portrays the heat of love, desire burning Medea. These passages recall Sappho's language – the sparkle of Anaktoria's face in fragment 16, the fluttering of desire in fragment 22, her heart excited and agitated in her breast in fragment 31. Such language becomes part of the poetic canon, with a long history; love produces physical symptoms, the contradictory experience of hot and cold, the heart jumping, the face pallid, then flushed. The language shows how Sappho lives on in the conventions representing someone, especially a woman, in love.

Medea's powers are eventually used for destruction as well as seduction. Medea leaves her family behind, according to legend dismembering her younger brother and distributing his body parts in the sea to foil her pursuers. She boils Jason's enemy Pelias, convincing the king's daughters that this will rejuvenate him. She murders her rival, Jason's new bride, with a hideous flesh-eating poison and then kills her own two sons as revenge for his betrayal. The bodily effects of eros, detailed by Sappho and adopted by Euripides and by Apollonios Rhodios, have a long, sometimes contradictory legacy in the poetic tradition, and can create sympathy for their victims that may turn to repulsion.

The poets of the Hellenistic age acknowledged Sappho; among them were other women poets, mentioned earlier. As the power of Rome began to expand, first dominating all of Italy, then defeating the Carthaginians in Sicily and north Africa, finally moving north to Britain and eastwards into Greece, Asia Minor and finally Egypt, an empire was created that both conquered and was conquered by Greek culture. Antipater of Sidon, in Phoenicia, of the second century BCE, spent the end of his life in Rome, and wrote among other works an epitaph addressing the 'Aiolian earth' where Sappho was buried, calling her the 'mortal' muse and asking the Fates why they had not made her immortal. Speaking in the voice of Sappho, he says: 'I so far surpassed women in poetry as Homer surpassed men.' Tullius Laurea, a former slave freed by the Roman orator Cicero, also wrote a poem in Greek addressing a stranger passing by Sappho's Aiolian tomb, using Sappho's voice: 'do not say that I am dead ... if you judge me by the Muses, know that I escaped the darkness of Hades, and there will be no sun, no day, without the name of the lyric poet Sappho.' Other writers on these matters, often within the huge field of Roman domination, attribute the invention of specific metres to Sappho and call her the inventor of a particular type of lyre; they use Sappho as an example of elegant and spectacular style, of charm, of invocation of the many gods.

Rome began as a village on a hill and became the master of a great empire, an empire which up until the time of Octavian, heir of Julius Caesar and the first emperor, first among equals, the 'princeps', was ruled as a republic by an aristocracy, an oligarchy that only grudgingly admitted new men into the governing class. After the conquest of Greece, Roman intellectuals, always conscious of rude beginnings, paradoxically tempted by but also wary of the sophistication of the Greeks of the mainland, the islands, southern Italy and Sicily and African Egypt, took up various attitudes in relation to Greek culture. They appropriated it in the form of educated Greek slaves and dependent artists and intellectuals; some judged it as decadent and soft, unworthy to be embraced by a nation of farmers and soldiers. Sometimes looking back to Greek models showed cultural sophistication and erudition; sometimes it was judged as falling prey to the luxuriousness and self-indulgence that conservative Roman thinkers attributed to the Greeks. Ennius, who wrote in the third and second centuries BCE, came from a region of Italy where Greek culture dominated, and wrote in many poetic genres, using Greek metres. The second-century BCE Roman dramatists Plautus and Terence, born as a slave in Africa, based their comedies on Greek originals, especially the plays of Menander.

The Roman poet Catullus, who lived in the first century BCE, was deeply influenced by Hellenistic poetry, especially the work of Kallimakhos, a contemporary of Apollonios Rhodios who wrote intricate, difficult, allusive poetry. Catullus, who lived from about 84 to 54 BCE, in a time of great turmoil as the Roman republic was being torn apart by powerful rivals contesting for domination of the state, was part of a new movement of self-conscious writers who acknowledged their debt to the Greeks. He attacks Julius Caesar in his work, Caesar who attempted to control Rome and its empire and was later assassinated in 44 BCE. Along with political poems and scornful, mocking poems ridiculing various contemporaries, Catullus shows himself to be an attentive and inventive reader of Sappho.

Many of his poems are addressed to, or speak of, a woman he calls 'Lesbia'. The later writer Apuleius, author of the wonderful novel *The Golden Ass*, identifies Lesbia as Clodia, portrayed by Cicero as a married, promiscuous and dangerously manipulative woman. Is Catullus' naming of his mistress, his lover, his fantasy addressee, a homage to the archaic Greek Sappho or an allusion to the woman's sexual appetites, which encompassed what we now would call 'lesbian' desire? Although earlier scholars attempted to follow the progress of an actual affair between Catullus and Clodia through a biographical tracing of the content of his poems, as was done once upon a time with the works of Sappho as well, more recent readers have found in the poet's invention of this Lesbia ways of expressing eroticism, misogyny and an exploration of relations of dominance and submission, obligation and reciprocity, characteristic of elite Roman society. Poem 5, addressed to Lesbia, represents her as sharing with him a private erotic world:

> Let us live, my Lesbia, and love, and take the talk of judgemental old men as worth but a penny. Suns can set and return. To us, when once our brief light has set, remains only one perpetual night to be slept. Give me a thousand kisses, then a hundred, then another thousand, a second hundred, another thousand, then a hundred, then, when we have come to many thousands, we will confound our counting, so we won't know the number, nor can any wicked person hex us, when he knows that our kisses are so many.
>
> (Translated by F. W. Cornish, revised by G. P. Goold)

Using the language of business, of accounting, Catullus asks his Lesbia to baffle the disapproving elders who sit in judgement on his extravagances. Demonstrating the mobile libido, moving from woman to man, to slave boy or man or girl or woman, of the elite male of antiquity, Catullus wrote a similar poem addressed to the boy, or man, Juventius, whose honeyed eyes the poet would kiss 300,000 times, if allowed, nor would he ever be satisfied, even if the crop of kisses were denser than ears of ripe corn. Another poem jealously refers to the handsome Lesbius, in the masculine form of the name given to the mistress; Lesbia prefers Lesbius to Catullus.

Lesbia, and allusions to Sappho, appear frequently in Catullus' works; he writes with envy of his lady's pet sparrow, who plays in her lap and pecks at her finger, the sparrow, bird of Aphrodite, recalling the sparrows that draw the goddess' golden chariot down from Olympus in Sappho's fragment 1. He calls the mistress of Caecilius, who dotes on this fellow poet, whose marrow burns with erotic fire, *Sapphica puella/ Musa doctior*, 'a girl more learned than the Sapphic Muse'. One of Catullus' wedding poems, a choral song to the god Hymen, Hymenaios, has echoes of Sappho, with reference to the hyacinth flower, to Hesperus, the evening star, and to the flower that grows up in a fenced garden, that fades when torn by a nail, likened to the maiden who has been deflowered. In a longer poem commemorating the wedding of Peleus and Thetis that brought their son Akhilleus into the world, Catullus describes the less happy union of Theseus and Ariadne; his description of the first ship passing over the sea, over the head of the Nereids, daughters of the sea god Nereus, finds Thetis in amazement, with her sisters, standing out from the sea to watch this extraordinary thing, and Peleus burning with love for the sea creature. Ariadne conceives a burning love, in her very marrow, for Theseus, and she grows pale with love. Sappho's vocabulary of the impact of desire on the body persists in these poems, layered with references to archaic Greek songs, to Euripides and to Apollonios' descriptions of the love-sick Medea. Such language will find a place later in Virgil's *Aeneid* and its account of the Carthaginian queen, Dido, who dies for love of Aeneas, founder of Rome.

Elsewhere, Catullus refers to Sappho's 'bittersweet' love. He 'burns', and in a poetic rage at his Lesbia, the poet denounces her for prostitution in the crossroads and alleys of Rome. The most extraordinary homage to Sappho, however, is Catullus' poem 51, which is a translation into Latin, and perhaps into heterosexuality, of Sappho's fragment 31, 'He appears to me, that man, an equal to the gods...' This is Catullus' 'translation':

> That man to me seems to be equal to a god,
> he, if it is permitted to say so, even to transcend the gods,
> who sitting across from you, over and over
>   gazes at you and hears

> you sweetly laughing; wretched, this
> all my senses tears from me; for at once
> when I look at you, Lesbia, nothing is left to me
>
> ...
>
> but my tongue goes numb, and down through my limbs
> a fine flame glides; with their own din
> my ears ring; my eyes are covered
> in a double night.
>
> idleness, Catullus, for you is troublesome;
> in idleness you revel and exult too much.
> Idleness before now both kings and wealthy
> cities has destroyed.
>
> (Translated by F. W. Cornish, revised by G. P. Goold)

The last stanza refers to *otium*, 'idleness', and it is unclear if it continues to translate a variant fragmentary ending of Sappho's poem, or constitutes a self-conscious reprimand of the poet to himself. But here Catullus even uses Sappho's metre, the 'Sapphic stanza', while making the scene of a woman watching a beloved woman with a man, into a scene of a man watching his beloved, Lesbia, with another man. It is a complex homage to the Lesbian poet, which acknowledges his predecessor, deploys her verse, her imagery, even her forms of alliteration, repeating words, and sounds that echo through the lines, engaging in a sort of poetic transvestism as he constructs a love poem to a woman; yet he is a man, a man who reproaches himself for idleness.

Catullus died before Octavian, Julius Caesar's heir, defeated Mark Antony in 31 BCE and began to set himself up as the sole effective ruler, the first of the emperors of Rome. In the new world of empire, poets were drawn into the transformation of culture launched by Augustus, as Octavian came to be known. And they sometimes expressed ambivalence or even outrage at the loss of republican freedoms. Virgil died before finishing his great epic poem the *Aeneid*, describing the founding of Rome by the Trojan

Aeneas, but his account of the journey from Troy, echoing Homer's *Iliad* and *Odyssey* and Apollonios Rhodios' *Argonautica*, has been seen recently less as an unqualified celebration of Augustus' domination, more as a nuanced assessment of the losses incurred in the necessary establishment of Roman imperial power. Virgil's Dido, an abandoned lover like Medea, burns with Sapphic, Euripidean, Apollonian love for his hero Aeneas.

Horace, solicited by Augustus' friend, ally and impresario of cultural support, did celebrate the regime, but also treasured a quiet life in a country villa, acquired under the patronage of Augustus, out of the flux of conflict that surrounded Augustus' consolidation of his reign. In his odes, Horace expresses to a tree his gratitude for a narrow escape from death, when that tree seems to have fallen on his head. He gladly lists those in the underworld whom he might have glimpsed, had the tree brained him: Proserpina queen of the dead, 'Sappho complaining on her Aiolian lyre about her girl companions'. In the land of the dead, Sappho is still singing, although Horace has not joined her, yet. In a verse letter addressed to his patron Maecenas in 20 BCE, Horace responds to criticism of his earlier *Odes* and *Epodes*, and argues that other poets have abjectly modelled themselves on their Greek predecessors in poetry, but he does otherwise. He begins epistle 19 of the first book of letters with the claim that no poem written by a poet who drinks water, not wine, can please or have a long life. Other poets make up 'a slavish herd'. He himself is a leader, claiming to have been the first to show to the Romans the iambic metres of the Greek island of Paros, home of Archilochus. And he justifies his practice by allusion to other archaic Greek poets:

> Masculine Sappho tempers the Muse with the metrical foot of Archilochus.
> Alcaeus tempers his, though his themes and order differ ...

These Lesbian poets, though singing 600 years before, offer metres, themes, love of wine, that inspire the Roman poet. The reference to *mascula Sappho*, 'masculine/male/manly/virile/vigorous/superior', has stimulated scholarly controversy. Is Horace referring to Sappho's reputation as a poet, as the tenth Muse, as a poet ranking among the greatest of male poets? Or is this an offhand allusion to her sexual preference for women and girls? In either case, Horace acknowledges the enabling precedent of Sappho's poetry and lists her among the great ancestors whom he honours with his own verse. And he boasts that he scorns the judgement of the *grammatici*, the professors of literature!

Other Latin writers refer to Sappho, some locating her among the poetic greats of the Greek past, others referring to what they represent as the 'indecency' of her love. A papyrus from the late second or early third century CE gives a brief biography, including the fact that 'she was denounced by some for being *ataktos* ("disorderly"), in her way of life, and *gynaikerastria* ("a lover of women")'. The French philosopher and historian Michel Foucault and others have described the process by which, in the common era, as ancient philosophers and elite thinkers developed new attitudes to the body and eros, a scepticism grew concerning traditional sexuality. Philosophical schools began to advocate celibacy, and there was in some circles the development of a disdain for physical contact. Marriage between one man and one woman was urged, as the best way to master sexual desire. All these tendencies were eventually reinforced with the institutional triumph of Christianity over paganism. But it may be that the heterosexualisation of Sappho contributed to or was influenced by these changes.

The great poet Ovid, one of the most brilliant writers of the Roman period, lived in the time of Augustus and spanned the period we now improbably break into BCE and CE, from 43 BCE to 17 CE. He wrote in many genres – love poetry, a manual of seduction, a calendar of the Roman year, letters from exile, and an extraordinary epic poem, *Metamorphoses*, in which he includes the making of the universe, Greek epic and Roman history, Greek and Roman myth and ancient philosophy of many tendencies, ending it all with a declaration that his name will never die. He was exiled by Augustus for crimes unknown, possibly sexual indiscretions, and spent his last years yearning to return from what is now Romania. He also wrote a fascinating text called the *Heroides*, which became definitive for the legacy of Sappho. The poetic letters that make up this work probably belong to the earlier period of his life, the time of love poetry and the *Ars Amatoria*, the seduction manual, although some scholars think the later letters in the *Heroides*, letters 16–21, were published after the *Metamorphoses*. The book collects the letters allegedly written by famous and legendary women to their absent lovers or husbands. There are letters from Penelope, wife of the wandering Ulysses, as the Romans called him, from the Carthaginian queen, Dido, ablaze with love, on the verge of suicide, in an agony of yearning for her departed lover, Aeneas, about to sail off to found Rome. She ends her letter with her epitaph, accusing Aeneas of her death. Medea writes to Jason, threatening him as she recounts their history together; no enemy of Medea will go unpunished. These letters have an operatic quality, like the arias of later sopranos, who in extended and intense soliloquies express yearning and even despair in the most extravagant of tones. The last of the first 15 letters is a letter from 'Sappho', which, in a sort of theatrical monologue posing as a letter, expresses to the supposed recipient Phaon her frantic and undying love.

This Sappho is the one bequeathed to posterity, for many centuries the definitive, forlorn, love-struck and suicidal poet who has given up the love of women for an unrequited passion for a young man. 'Sappho' here begins by addressing her absent lover, who has abandoned her, travelling from Greece to Sicily, while Sappho herself burns no less than the fires of the Sicilian volcano Etna. She has changed from the lyric mode to the elegiac, the verse form used in Rome by amatory poets. Elegy is the form, she says, suited for weeping, and paradoxically, she weeps as she burns. The girls she once pursued mean nothing to her now, and she names Anaktoria, Cydro and Atthis among hundreds more. Only young and beautiful Phaon is the object of her desire. And though she is short, not beautiful, and dark, she has won praise for the beauty of her songs. Like birds of differing colour, they could mate. Once upon a time she read her verses to him and he kissed her. But he now pursues the girls of Sicily. Sappho begs help from the goddess of Eryx, a settlement in Sicily, which had a temple dedicated to Astarte, the Phoenician form of the goddess, and in her manifestations as Aphrodite and Venus, an Italian goddess who was eventually identified with the Greek Aphrodite. She recalls the death of her father when she was six, and her useless brother, caught in love by a prostitute, now a pirate full of hate for Sappho his sister. She no longer bothers to adorn herself. She fears the goddesses will steal Phaon. She writes and weeps, and the teardrops blot her lines. He has left her nothing. In lines that recall her fragment 31, she describes being unable to weep, unable to speak, frozen with grief. Her brother delights in her misery. She dreams of Phaon and fondles him in her dreams. Modestly, she glides over what must be an allusion to masturbation, or nocturnal orgasm: 'More I am ashamed to tell, but all takes place, and I am pleasured, and cannot be abstemious.'

The Sappho of Ovid's letter goes on to describe how she raves, maddened, through the woods, finding the spot on which she once lay with Phaon. A naiad, a water nymph, accosts her by a spring, and advises her to go to the white rock of Leukas, in north-west Greece, where the god Apollo looks out across the sea. There Deucalion, the only man to survive the great flood sent by Zeus to punish humankind, threw himself over the rock, inflamed with love for Pyrrha, the only woman. He survived the fall unharmed, and his agonising desire left him, as he was freed from love's fires. The naiad links the spot with Actium, a name that resounds in Roman history, since from this cliff above the sea Octavian watched the battle in 31 BCE between his forces and the fleet of Antony and Cleopatra, and saw Antony abandon the fight in pursuit of the fleeing Cleopatra back to Egypt, which led to suicide for both. Sappho promises to seek out the spot, to jump, and asks Amor, 'Love', to carry her on his wings as she leaps, lest she die. She leaves the tortoise shell of her lyre to Apollo, god of music and the muses, and beneath it an epigram: 'Gratefully I, the poetess Sappho, set down my lyre for you, Phoebus, appropriate to me, appropriate to you.' Yet immediately she asks why she is being sent to Actium, when Phaon could be an Apollo for her and rescue her in her distress. But she has lost her powers of eloquence; her lyre is silenced. The daughters of Lesbos, whom she has loved, infamously, are commanded to cease listening to her lyre. Phaon has destroyed all that they once loved. Bring him back and their singer will return. He gave force to her genius; he tore it away. She asks finally if her prayers have any effect. She commands him to weigh anchor, promising that Venus, born from the sea, makes way for the lover. Cupid will steer the boat and set the sails. But if Phaon chooses to fly from Sappho, may he at least answer her letter, telling her of his choice, so that her destiny may be sought in the Leucadian waters. The power of the letter struck readers, even though the authorship of Ovid himself was called into question. Ovid's skills of characterising a person, a personality, through her words, seemed evident, and made of this Sappho a vivid, desperate, victimised heroine. She had given up her disorderly, infamous love of girls, and joined the honourable host of ancient women yearning for absent, abandoning, unfaithful male lovers.

Sappho survived for centuries as the maddened heterosexual of Ovid's text. Her poetry gradually disappeared. The library of Alexandria, which contained the supposed nine books of Sappho's songs, one for each of the Muses, was damaged by fire several times after its great flourishing. Scrolls were lost, some possibly destroyed because of their content, because of Christian disapproval of ancient mores. The recorded words of Jesus himself nowhere express any hostility towards homoeroticism; in fact some scholars of the first-century CE context of his life, and of the non-canonical books of the New Testament, those books not selected for inclusion in one of several versions of the Bible, argue that Jesus had a 'beloved', a male lover. But Paul, one of the founders of institutionalised Christianity, adheres more closely to readings of the Hebrew Bible that condemn homosexuality, although these too have been disputed. The Hebrew Bible itself, a complex, layered, many-voiced text, contains contradictory messages about this issue; David and Jonathan, for example, love one another, Jonathan 'gives his heart to David', and each loves the other as dearly as he loves himself. On the other hand, in the context of condemning cult practices of the neighbours of the ancient Israelites, including child sacrifice, the 'holiness code' of Leviticus prohibits sexual acts between men, as well as male–female intercourse during menstruation and adultery. In his letter to the Romans, Paul condemns those who fail to honour his god, those who saw his power, who should have known better. They are condemned for worshipping images. Because of their worship and service to the creature rather than the creator, Paul asserted, the god gave them up in the lusts of their hearts to impurity, to degrading passions, to intercourse 'against nature, or convention', and men were consumed with passion for one another. Such condemnation touches not only on the objects of desire of those idolaters who were punished by the god but also on excesses of sexual practice, a failure to master the self and an over-indulgence in sexual pleasures. For these malefactors, clearly not just the 'gentile', so-called pagan Romans, but also Paul's Jewish audience, disastrous consequences ensued. Christianity came to condemn same-sex eroticism, although even there some have argued for early church libertinism and same-sex unions.

In any case, the legacy of ancient literary texts that celebrated the varieties of ancient sexuality often conflicted with official Christian teachings, and many of the great works of antiquity were dismembered, mutilated or discarded. Deliberate or not, losses occurred to most of the texts of the ancient Greek world during the so-called 'Dark Ages' and 'Middle Ages' in Europe, when the Roman Empire, which had been gradually Christianised, fell victim to invasions from more northerly peoples. Codices, bound sheets like those of modern books, replaced scrolls, some preserved in monasteries, others buried in Egyptian sands, or in dumps. Papyrus had been used in Egypt to form the 'cartonnage' wrappings and funerary masks of mummies and some ancient papyri have been retrieved from these sources, of which more in subsequent chapters. But in the twelfth century CE, that is, 1700 years after her lifetime, Johannes Tzetzes, a classicising writer in Christian Constantinople, commenting on the metres of Pindar, acknowledged in verse that Sappho and the things of Sappho, the lyre and the songs, have come to the ruin of time, so he must offer, as precedent, other verses to his reader.

IV

TRYING TO TRANSLATE SAPPHO

IN THIS CHAPTER, I first discuss the 'translation' of the figure of Sappho, focusing on the ways in which her life was understood and used in the period after the Middle Ages. Then I look at traditions of literary translation, as her surviving poems were rendered into modern languages, especially into English. The concluding sections of this chapter will consider the project of translation of Sappho that I undertook with the poet John Daley. I will concentrate especially on the three most recently discovered poems, which have shed much new light on Sappho – Sappho ageing, Sappho as a sister.

Much of classical culture disappeared after the fall of the Roman Empire in the fifth century CE. Although Christians were urged to take the best of this legacy, as the Israelites had carried with them the treasures of the Egyptians as they departed for their promised land, there were controversies about the best, with philosophy surviving better than the erotic poetry of classical Greece and Rome. A few fragmentary poems of Sappho only very gradually came to light. The first poem was preserved in the text of Dionysios of Halikarnassos, published in the sixteenth century; fragment 31, contained in the treatise *On the Sublime*, attributed to Longinus, was copied into a medieval manuscript in the tenth century CE, and also not printed until the sixteenth century, when the European Renaissance had come to recognise the divide that separated them from the ancient cultures of Greece and Rome and sought to incorporate them into a re-naissance, a 're-birth' of this heritage. The influential man of letters Nicolas Boileau translated fragment 31 into French in 1674, and this translation, reaching a wider audience, may have had its impact on developments in lyric poetry in seventeenth-century France.

Other shreds, other fragments of Sappho's nine books of poetry emerged in the course of time, found in the works of other ancient authors for the most part, in passages that illustrated metres or that sought to clarify words that had become unintelligible over time. The great trove of papyri uncovered in the nineteenth and twentieth centuries in Egypt, especially in the rubbish heaps of the city of Oxyrhynchus, brought most of the fragments. Oxyrhynchus was a prosperous city during the Hellenistic and Roman periods, named after a variety of fish said to have devoured the penis of Osiris, the Egyptian god killed and dismembered by his brother Set and recovered, except for this particular part, by his sister/wife the goddess Isis. The residents of Oxyrhynchus had in antiquity discarded huge quantities of papyrus in the city's dump, in a relatively dry zone untouched by the annual flooding of the Nile. Much of the papyrus concerned the administration of the town, or consisted of legal documents of its citizens; very few of the fragments contained literary or philosophical texts. In 1896 the Oxford archaeologists Bernard Grenfell and Arthur Hunt began excavating the city's dumping grounds and found a vast trove of ancient texts, including fragments of the poet Pindar and the playwrights Sophocles, Euripides and Menander, and portions of the work of the great geometrician Euclid. There were also bits, fragments, shreds of papyrus that had copies, in various stages of readability, of Sappho and Alkaios. Scholars who received the bounty of these excavations have devoted their careers to the careful separation of leaves of papyrus, the attempt to preserve as much as possible of the delicate vegetable matter, since papyrus was formed by the flattening of the pith of the papyrus plant, and to the analysis of the writing on the surface, often badly eroded, torn and difficult to interpret. Even when reading of the texts was possible, these scholars found broken edges and incomprehensible passages, sometimes owing to slips of the pen by ancient copyists, who lived hundreds of years after the archaic period of Sappho and even of the classical authors. Some of the papyri became valuable commodities and were sold. Some, stored in European libraries for years, undeciphered, have yielded new poems, or fuller versions of poems for which there was only a very partial understanding.

One of the few early modern poets to come to terms with the homoeroticism of Sappho's verse was the English John Donne, who in the seventeenth century wrote a poem entitled 'Sapho to Philaenis' that constitutes a sort of response to the tradition of Ovid. It comes in a set of letters to 'several personages', is followed by a letter to Ben Jonson, a contemporary seventeenth-century writer, and includes a poem written in Donne's erudite Latin. Donne's are 'epistolary' poems, that is, in the form of letters like those written by Ovid, who used the voices of various heroines to chastise and plead with unresponsive lovers. But Donne restores the female–female eroticism of Sappho herself. Rather than turning away from the love of girls and women to the man Phaon, Donne's 'heroine' rejects Phao, as he calls him, and speaks to her lover, in language as powerful as that of the twentieth-century feminist Luce Irigaray's 'When Our Lips Speak Together', in *This Sex Which Is Not One*.

> Where is that holy fire, which *Verse* is said
> To have? is that inchanting force decai'd?
> *Verse* that drawes *Natures* works, from *Natures* law,
> Thee, her best worke, to her worke cannot draw.
> Have my teares quench'd my old *Poetique* fire;
> Why quench'd they not as well, that of *desire*?
> Thoughts, my mindes creatures, often are with thee,
> But I, their maker, want their libertie.
> Onely thine image, in my heart, doth sit,
> But that is waxe, and fires environ it.
> My fires have driven, thine have drawne it hence;
> And I am rob'd of *Picture*, *Heart*, and *Sense*.

Dwells with me still mine irksome *Memory*,
Which, both to keepe, and lose, grieves equally.
That tells me'how faire thou art: Thou art so faire,
As, *gods*, when *gods* to thee I doe compare,
Are grac'd thereby; And to make blinde men see,
What things *gods* are, I say they'are like to thee.
For, if we justly call each silly *man*
A *litle world*, What shall we call thee then?
Thou art not soft, and clear, and strait, and faire,
As *Down*, as *Stars*, *Cedars*, and *Lillies* are,
But thy right hand, and cheek, and eye, only
Are like thy other hand, and cheek, and eye.
Such was my *Phao*'awhile, but shall be never,
As thou, wast, art, and, oh, maist be ever.
Here lovers sweare in their *Idolatrie*,
That I am such; but *Griefe* discolours me.
And yet I grieve the lesse, lest *Griefe* remove
My beauty, and make me'unworthy of thy love.
Plaies some soft boy with thee, oh there wants yet
A mutuall feeling which should sweeten it.
His chinne, a thorny hairy'unevennesse
Doth threaten, and some daily change possesse.
Thy body is a naturall *Paradise*,
In whose self, unmanur'd, all pleasure lies,
Nor needs *perfection*; why shouldst thou than
Admit the tillage of a harsh rough man?
Men leave behind them that which their sin shows,
And are as theeves trac'd, which rob when it snowes.
But of our dallyance no more signes there are,
Then *fishes* leave in streames, or *Birds* in aire.
And betweene us all sweetnesse may be had;
All, all that *Nature* yields, or *Art* can adde.
My two lips, eyes, thighs, differ from thy two,
But so, as thine from one another doe;

> And, oh, no more; the likeness being such,
> Why should they not alike in all parts touch?
> Hand to strange hand, lippe to lippe none denies;
> Why should they brest to brest, or thigh to thighs?
> Likenesse begets such strange selfe flatterie,
> That touching my self, all seems done to thee.
> My selfe I'embrace, and mine owne hands I kiss,
> And amorously thanke my selfe for this.
> Me, in my glasse, I call thee; But alas,
> When I would kisse, teares dimme mine *eyes*, and *glasse*,
> O cure this loving madnesse, and restore
> Me to mee; thee, my *halfe*, my *all*, my *more*.
> So may thy cheeks red outweare scarlet dye,
> And their white, whitenesse of the *Galaxy*,
> So may thy mighty', amazing beauty move
> *Envy*'in all *women*, and in all men, *love*,
> And so be *change*, and *sicknesse*, farre from thee,
> As thou by comming neere, keep'st them from me.
>
> (John Donne, 'Sapho to Philaenis')

Donne restores to Sappho the eros of lesbianism, the rejection of a bristly, unappealing male body, and assimilates Sappho's love for Philaenis to self-love, autoeroticism, masturbation. Philaenis was mentioned in various ancient texts; the Roman Martial describes her as an athlete, as hypermasculine and having a marked taste for young girls, of which Martial clearly disapproved. Another Philaenis was supposed to be the author of erotic verse. Possibly a purely literary construct, she was nonetheless not a contemporary of Sappho, but appears also in the *Greek Anthology* of later poets, Aiskhrion recording her voice in an inscription on a tomb on a cliff over the sea, a voice speaking to passing sailors, swearing that she was not a prostitute. In another poem, Dioskorides refutes the attribution of obscenity to her. And a dialogue attributed to Lucian (born about 120 CE), but possibly written in the fourth century CE, *Erotes* or *Amores*, *Affairs of the Heart*, to be considered more fully in the next chapter, names Philaenis in an argument defending women's right to same-sex love, in parallel with men's pleasures with one another. These remnants of the reputation of 'Philaenis' may have appealed to the erudite cleric John Donne.

Donne's poem begins with the 'I', Sapho, fearing that her tears have quenched her poetic fire, and echoes Sappho's own verse when she says: 'Thou art so faire,/ as, gods, when gods to thee I doe compare,/ Are grac'd thereby'. To explain to blind men what gods are, she likens them to her lover Philaenis. She rejects the conventions of erotic verse: her lover is not soft and clear and straight and fair, but her right hand and cheek and eye resemble her left, as the theme of mirroring symmetry arises. This Sapho once loved 'Phao', but no more. If Philaenis is somewhere, playing with a boy, they lack 'a mutuall feeling'. He has a thorny, hairy, uneven chin, while Philaenis' body is 'a naturall *Paradise* ... [where] all pleasure lies'. Intercourse between a man and woman, presumed illicit, leaves behind the sign of their sin, a child, just as a robber leaves his footprints in the snow. But the intercourse of Sapho and her lover leaves no trace behind; it is like the gliding of a fish through a stream, or the flight of birds. The resemblance of the two women's bodies is like the poet's limbs' resemblance to one another; why, if hands and lips can touch with no one finding fault, should not breasts and thighs? Here Donne goes beyond the orator of Lucian's dialogue, who seems to support fairness in the right of women to make love to one another, but still condemns such behaviour. Donne, taking on the voice of Sappho as Catullus once did, engages in a transvestism, a transgendering, as he imagines himself not to be Catullus replacing Sappho's speaker, but rather as the woman herself, imagining love-making with another woman. The poem moves to a moment of self-pleasuring that recalls the Sappho of Ovid's letter. Here the character Sapho gazes into the mirror and calls what she sees 'thee', 'you', 'Philaenis'. But her yearning for the absent lover overwhelms her, and tears cloud her gaze. She begs that Philaenis cure her madness and restore her to herself. Her own identity, mingled with that of her double, her love, mirrored in the glass, diffuses into the other, whom she calls, emphatically, 'my *halfe*, my *all*, my *more*'. Philaenis is not simply her other half, but, in a complex mathematical figure, all of her, and more. If Philaenis will return to her, then her lover will fend off change, the change, and sickness, love sickness. This Sapho, rather than the chaotic, disturbed Sappho of Ovid's *Heroides*, is a brilliant poet, rhetorically adept, ironic, capable of the most subtle of wordplay, in control of her letter.

British literary history contains other allusions to Sappho. Harriette Andreadis, in a chapter in the collective volume edited by Ellen Greene, *Re-Reading Sappho*, entitled 'Sappho in early modern England', describes the ways in which the figure of the archaic Greek poet was present even before the discovery of many of her fragments in the nineteenth century. She summarises her findings:

> [T]here were three primary modes of representing Sappho in early modern England: she was portrayed as a mythologized figure who acts the suicidal abandoned woman in the Ovidian tale of Sappho and Phaon; she was used as the first example of female poetic excellence, most often with a disclaimer of any sexuality (or what Abraham Cowley called 'ill manners'); and she was presented as an early exemplar of 'unnatural' or monstrous sexuality.
>
> (Andreadis, in *Re-Reading Sappho*, p. 106)

Andreadis cites translations of Ovid's *Heroides*, in which the sexual preferences of Sappho seem to oscillate. John Lyly wrote a late-sixteenth-century play entitled *Sapho and Phao*; here Sapho, perhaps in reference to Queen Elizabeth I, successfully controls the disruptive erotic forces of Venus and Cupid. In the seventeenth century, references to the greatness of Sappho, the tenth muse, proliferated as forms of complimentary address to female poets. Katherine Philips (1632–64), for example, was called 'the new Sappho'; some readers find homoerotic themes in her verses that speak of intense female friendship, although contemporaries calling her by the name of her illustrious predecessor may simply allude to her excellence rather than her sexual proclivities. Andreadis also discusses the place of 'tribadism', from the Greek word *tribo*, 'rub', in medical literature of the early modern period. An early anatomy lists both Philaenis and Sappho as among those who practised such 'carnal Copulation' with each other, and in the translation of the Latin, these women are called 'Rubsters'. Texts written in the seventeenth century, by women, such as the Duchess of Newcastle's play *The Convent of Pleasure*, of 1668, and others, depict female same-sex desire. Aphra Behn wrote a poem entitled 'To the Fair Clarinda, Who Made Love to Me, Imagined More than Woman', published in 1688.

Alan Bray's ground-breaking book *Homosexuality in Renaissance England*, published by Gay Men's Press in 1982, describes the unfettered practice of male homosexuality in the period, which, though considered 'sodomy', was not considered to be performed by 'homosexuals' per se, who emerged as an identifiable group only later, with the gradual medicalisation and pathologisation of various sexual practices that did not conform to the heterosexual ideal. Women's friendships, idealisation, even adoration, were not necessarily seen as problematic in early modern England, but the pleasures of the body were eventually relegated to medical texts and to a judgement condemning forbidden, transgressive forms of love-making between women. Alexander Pope (1688–1744) translated Ovid's fifteenth letter from the *Heroides* as 'Sappho to Phaon', published in 1712, using rhymed couplets. His Sappho, learning of her abandonment by her lover, falls to pieces:

> Like some sad statue, speechless, pale, I stood,
> Grief chill'd my breast, and stopt my freezing blood.
> No sigh to rise, no tear had power to flow,
> Fix'd in a stupid lethargy of woe.

Pope echoes the customary alternation of temperature, a legacy from Sappho's own fragment 31, even as he fits Ovid's verse into the order of English rhyme and metre. His Sappho, once again, throws herself into the sea: 'To raging seas unpitied I'll remove,/ And either cease to live or cease to love!'

In the European context as well, Sappho came to be known as the poet defined by her unrequited love for Phaon. The best account of the 'reception' of Sappho in continental Europe comes in the book *Fictions of Sappho: 1546–1937* by Joan DeJean, published in 1989. DeJean catalogues century by century the figure of Sappho in the French literary world. Even before the translation of the few fragments available in the period, the translation of Ovid's *Heroides* in the early sixteenth century affects the French understanding of Sappho in the years that follow. DeJean describes a French Sappho, at first, in the sixteenth century, when Sappho's poetry was first recovered, as she was permitted a polymorphous desire; yet the verses, and their expressed desire of the writer for a woman, are appropriated by male poets, as Sappho presides at the very beginnings of the modern French literary tradition. Sappho is above all a person in love with a woman, and the influence of Catullus' reading and rewriting of Sappho is central. At the beginnings of the novel, in the seventeenth century, the French follow the lead of Ovid's heroine, and efface the homoeroticism in the Greek poet's verse. In Racine's *Phèdre*, a version of Euripides' *Hippolytus*, the heroine, tragically enamoured of her stepson, speaks of her passion in language that recalls Sappho's fragment 31, translated by Boileau: the dramatic character says: 'I see him, I blush, I turn pale.' Phèdre's soul is troubled, her eyes no longer see, she cannot speak, her whole body freezes, is paralysed, burns. The complex identifications between the tragic woman speaking and the male writer ventriloquising her prefigure Flaubert's comment, '*Madame Bovary, c'est moi.*' And according to DeJean the cultural space that might have allowed for female poetic authorship recedes, and Sappho becomes the passionate and suicidal heroine written by a male writer, 'sexually pitiable' (*Fictions of Sappho: 1546–1937*, p. 44). At the same time, Ovid's Sappho, ultimately derived from fragment 31, 'Sappho love-struck', provides a model for the inventions of the novel, the epistolary form, a novel in letters and the romance. Sappho becomes Sapo, a tragic heroine, and Madeleine de Scudéry, known to her generation as 'Sapho', begins to compose novels of romance with a new version of female heroism. Her women are passionate, illustrious women, no longer victims, but rather examples of literary power, and her Sappho is one of these *femmes illustres*. Her Phaon is faithful. De Scudéry's version of Sappho excited a fervent denunciation by Boileau, and his dismissal of the heroic Sappho triumphs.

In the eighteenth century, in DeJean's account, Sappho became a mother. She was represented as decidedly heterosexual and mother of her daughter Kleis, contented with her maternal role, or often, on the other hand, as a promiscuous widow, abandoning her motherly responsibilities for the sake of her (heterosexual) desire. At the same time, there were 'sapphic' literary texts that made no reference to the ancient Greek poet, but focused on 'lesbian' plots set in other contexts. The legend of her exile in Sicily during the political turmoil of Mytilene allows also for a fantasy of Sappho as an aristocratic *émigrée*, like those dispersed by the French Revolution of 1789, and paradoxically for a 'revolutionary' Sappho, overthrower of tyranny, as well. Her sexuality becomes once again a matter of contestation, as the medicalisation, pathologisation, of 'homosexuality' becomes part of a cultural turn towards governing potentially unruly populations by means of the emerging social sciences. As DeJean puts it in *Fictions of Sappho: 1546–1937* (p. 13):

> In the course of the nineteenth century in France, Sappho leaves behind the often modest and always timid heterosexuality in which she had been disguised for nearly a century to reemerge as a figure of highly charged sexuality, first a courtesan, later a (sometimes depraved, sometimes oversexed) lesbian.

The Austrian playwright Franz Grillparzer wrote a tragedy, *Sappho*, first performed in Vienna in 1818, which crystallises the portrait of the love-mad Sappho throwing herself into the sea because of unrequited love for Phaon, who in Grillparzer's version of the plot has fallen in love with a younger woman, Melitta. In the nineteenth century scholars in Germany also interested themselves in Sappho, claiming for themselves a priority in matters of philology, that is, the scientific study of antiquity, especially through the establishing of authoritative and accurate versions of ancient writing in ancient languages. Writers allowed for the phenomenon of an idealised masculine physicality, in representations of 'Greek love', man–boy, man–man love, and Greek men in this version of antiquity could be beautiful, soldierly and patriotic. But pederasty, same-sex male sexuality in ancient Greece, must be protected from any feminisation through association with sapphistry; virility and male–male passion become part of a German nationalist preoccupation. Such views have their affinities with the work of the English writer John Addington Symonds, who urged pederasty as a model for noble virility, likening it to medieval chivalry. Sappho even becomes an object of devotion, like that given to the virgin Mary, for male homosexuals.

In the presentation of Sappho by German philologists she became a 'schoolmistress', the serene guide of younger women in their education towards womanhood. Phaon persisted as a tantalising object of desire, but this Sappho was chaste. DeJean describes this phase of the 'translation', the reception, the making of a Sappho for modernity, as 'Christianisation'. This Sappho is redeemed, as she becomes a virgin priestess. The French version of Sappho was in the nineteenth century a more contradictory one; their Sappho was either pure and chaste, or a dissolute homosexual, an alienated modernist lesbian. The French revived the ancient claim that there were two Sapphos on archaic Lesbos, one a poet, musician and schoolmistress, the other a *hetaira*, a courtesan abandoned by Phaon. The struggle between these visions of Sappho came to exemplify the contrast between French and German nationalist appropriations of antiquity. Philology became a sort of metaphorical battleground. The Germans sanitised Sappho, resistant to what they saw as the lurid tendencies of the French; the French deemed German scholarship austere and tedious. Baudelaire, who found Roman antiquity most fascinating, made an exception and went to the Greeks when he published his 'Lesbos' in 1850; the first title for his volume of poetry *Les Fleurs du mal* was *Les Lesbiennes*. As the vocabulary of sexual taxonomy developed towards the end of the nineteenth century, Sappho once again became, in France at least, a 'homosexual' poet, a 'lesbian'. Paul Verlaine presents Sappho in a series of 'Sapphic' sonnets. In 1895 Pierre Louÿs, in *Les Chansons de Bilitis*, portrays 'Psappha' as a schoolmistress instructing the rustic girl Bilitis in the ways of female homoeroticism.

When in the twentieth century new fragments of the poems of Sappho came to light from papyrus lost for over 1,500 years, she emerged once again as a model of female authorship and of lesbianism in the modern sense. The poet Renée Vivien, the 'Muse of the Violets', lover of Natalie Barney among other women, set herself to learning Greek so that she could translate Sappho's verse and wrote poetry of her own inspired by the example of Sappho. DeJean finds fault with what she calls 'Vivien's morbid identification with Sappho' (*Fictions of Sappho: 1546–1937*, p. 250); Vivien's texts urge a mystical union among women and girls. Barney herself was part of the 'Sapho 1900' group, and published a text called *Cinq petits dialogues grecs*, *Five Little Greek Dialogues*, in 1909; the dialogues present 'Sapphism' as a cult experience, requiring of its female devotees a complete dedication to the circle of women, refusing any reproductive or political engagements with a wider world. These writings excited some condemnation, as other writers found fault with the insularity of the Sapphic circles and used patriotic and sexological arguments against female homosexuality. The argument continued in the years before and after World War I. The Belgian Marguerite Yourcenar, who wrote in French and lived with her lover Grace Frick for almost 50 years, and who in 1980 was the first woman admitted to the Académie française, translated Sappho's fragments. In her 1936 publication *Feux*, she wrote in a prose poem entitled 'Sappho ou le suicide' of a modern Sappho who was a trapeze artist. Her Phaon is a transvestite who resembles the young girl Sappho loves; this Sappho throws herself from the acrobatic heights, but fails to die and ends stretched out on the sand, 'like a drowned woman'. As she traces this history from the early modern period through twentieth-century modernity, DeJean portrays a complex, lengthy set of cultural negotiations around the figure of Sappho, whose status as a female writer inspired women throughout the period in France, in the composition of novels, plays and poetry, but whose sexuality was a matter of ongoing dispute.

Although DeJean's study ends in 1937, Sappho in France became a significant figure for the so-called 'French feminists' of the post-1968 generations, Monique Wittig, Hélène Cixous and others, to be discussed further in the next chapter. Wittig, a lesbian activist, author of an influential text, *Les Guérillères*, *The Women Warriors*, saw Sappho as her lone predecessor. Catherine Ecarnot's study of Wittig is entitled *L'Écriture de Monique Wittig: à la couleur de Sappho*. In Wittig and Sande Zeig's *Lesbian Peoples: Material for a Dictionary* (1980), the page dedicated to Sappho is blank. I will come back to these questions in the final chapter of this book, on 'queer' Sappho, but for now it is enough to note the place of Sappho in twentieth-century French feminist writings. The theorists, influenced by Lacan and Derrida, include Wittig and Cixous, as well as Luce Irigaray and Julia Kristeva, who overtly or not gesture towards an *écriture féminine*, a feminine, female writing that looks back to the earliest explorations of the figure of Sappho in French literary history, and to the writing of Sappho herself as it gradually revealed itself over many centuries.

In a marvellous book called *Victorian Sappho*, published in 1999, Yopie Prins gives a series of studies of the reception of Sappho in Britain. Its cover is a reproduction of Charles-Auguste Mengin's portrait of the poet, dark, melancholy and bare-breasted, an image which created some problems in its circulation, as it was considered to verge on the pornographic by some authorities. Prins traces a Sappho effect through the Victorian period, as philology uncovered more and more of the ancient legacy of Greece and Rome, and as homoeroticism, homosexuality and pederasty were acknowledged, especially in elite culture. Such works as Stephen Marcus' *The Other Victorians* (1966) and Frank Turner's *The Greek Heritage in Victorian Britain* (1981) in very different ways began to delineate the place of Victorian eroticism in the history of sexuality. The popular edition of Sappho's fragments produced in 1885 by Henry Thornton Wharton had a great impact on poetry of the later nineteenth century. In a series of brilliant readings, towards which I direct the reader, Prins discusses among other matters the lesbian couple Katherine Bradley and Edith Cooper, who lived together as a married couple in the second half of the nineteenth and early twentieth centuries, and published plays and poetry as 'Michael Field'. Another fascinating chapter concerns the works of Algernon Charles Swinburne, author of the unfinished novel *Lesbia Brandon*, which combines reference to Sappho and her island as well as the addressee and subject of some of Catullus' lyrics, but also to the Swinburnian interest in flogging, and which was not published during the lifetime of the author.

Prins analyses fragment 31, especially the figure of the 'broken tongue' of Sappho, and explores this image to describe the proliferation of Sapphos, the dissemination of a broken body, a broken 'corpus' of poetry. Sappho's work becomes both the cause and the effect of translation and, in the English tradition, a feminised point of perfect origin for the lyric tradition. Prins moves from the circulation of translations to the doubled work of Bradley and Cooper, 'Michael Field'. These two, aunt and niece, discovered

Sappho's fragment 2, the summoning of Aphrodite to an enchanted grove, and this place, this 'topos', became for them a field for writing, a space in which they could both imitate Sappho and call their doubled identity by a man's name. Swinburne wrote imitations of Sappho early in his career, 'Anactoria', for example, and 'Sapphics', published in 1866. He found a certain voice, even as a 'male lesbian', and was celebrated for these works; his naming of Sappho as 'name above all names' designated her as his lyric ancestor, himself as a figure of decline from her perfections. Prins focuses on Sappho's fragment 130:

> Eros, the limb-loosener, again stirs me
> like a sweet bitter irresistible creeping beast.

Swinburne's fixing on these lines, the power of Eros to destroy, to cause the disintegration of body and self, his fascination with metre and with Sapphic metre in general, led him to experimentation with the verse forms that for him duplicated the force of flagellation. His unpublished *Flogging Book*, 12 eclogues, is preceded by invocation to 'the Muse who presides over the Ceremony of Flagellation'. The apprentice poet learns his lesson through the rhythmic application of the lash: 'Most the Nurslings of the Muse require/ The Lash that sets their lyrick Blood on Fire,/ The Lash that ever when they cry keeps Time,/ When Stroke to Stroke responds in glowing Rhyme/ And still the humbled Bottom hails the Rod sublime' (cited by Prins, p. 152). This Victorian Hellenist, one of the greatest poets of the era, contradicts the philologists' vision of Sappho as pure priestess and schoolmistress. Prins goes on to discuss the sentimental poetry of some women poets of the age, 'poetesses' English and American who focused on the Ovidian legacy of Sappho the tragic victim of unrequited love, again and again produced post-scripts to Sappho, to her leap from the white cliff, and predicted their own oblivion.

Simon Goldhill's study *Victorian Culture and Classical Antiquity: Art, Opera, Fiction, and the Proclamation of Modernity*, published in 2011, includes a chapter on Sappho that focuses on paintings of the ancient poet in the long Victorian age. Emphasising the transgressive representations of 'touch' in some of these works of art, he points to the danger Sapphic desire poses to received ideas; the touch is not registered, not even really visible in the mentality of the period in question. Goldhill traces the reactions of the contemporary audience by analysing reviews in contemporary newspapers and magazines, including *Punch*. The painting of Lawrence Alma-Tadema called *Sappho*, exhibited in Britain's Royal Academy in 1881, he notes, 'opens a space where desire may be viewed, [yet] the response is either silence, or a careful turning of the head, or a retreat into humor' (p. 82).

'Reception' has come to mean not only the ways in which an ancient work of art was 'received' in a later period, how it was transmitted, what effects it had on that period, how it was understood, but also an examination of how the ways in which the ancient text, object, work of art, theory was received can transform our understanding of antiquity itself. In the twentieth century, for example, when scholars were affected by developments in the suffragist movement, the women's movement, in feminism, they looked at the women of antiquity in new ways, seeking out silent members of ancient communities, studying the ways in which gender relations worked in ancient societies, a topic that had been relatively neglected in earlier periods. The interest in sexuality and in varieties of sexuality that came to define a new field called the history of sexuality also transformed readings of ancient societies and works of art. I will discuss this further in the last chapter of the book, on queer theory, but for now it is important to note that the understanding of Sappho in the post-Renaissance world was for a long time focused on her death, on the romance of her suicide and on the ways in which she stood for passionate and doomed eros rather than for 'lesbianism'. Sappho was seen not just as an exemplary female poet, but also and perhaps especially as a tragic figure. Visual artists represented Sappho, often with Phaon, as in the work of the neo-classical painter David, who painted them together in 1809.

The American poet Hilda Doolittle (1886–1961), who published as H. D., was, among others, profoundly influenced by Sappho's fragments. As a young woman she met William Carlos Williams, Marianne Moore and Ezra Pound, to whom she was briefly engaged. After moving to London, she came to know the imagist poets and Pound championed her work. She had affairs with both women and men, and married the poet Richard Aldington, but her most enduring relationship was with Annie Winifred Ellerman, the English novelist known as 'Bryher', whose father, a shipowner and financier, was said at the time of his death in 1933 to be the richest Englishman who had ever lived. Bryher was involved in film-making; her Pool group made *Borderline* in 1930, starring H. D. and the great African American singer and political activist Paul Robeson. Bryher, like H. D., married and had male lovers, but they saw themselves as Lesbian lesbians as well; Bryher's memoir is entitled *The Heart to Artemis*. H. D.'s sensuous life was unconventional, full, complex and polymorphous, marked by attachments to lovers of both genders, and by erotic suffering, it seems. H. D. was analysed by Sigmund Freud, and later wrote of the experience in her *Tribute to Freud*. While attracted to Japanese poetry, and the *haiku*, H. D. along with the other imagists early on began to derive inspiration from classical Greek poetry, and especially the archaic lyrics of Sappho.

The most explicit acknowledgement of H. D.'s fascination with Sappho comes in the text entitled 'The wise Sappho', written in 1920 but published in 1982 by City Lights Books, from a manuscript in the Beinecke Rare Book and Manuscript Library at Yale University. H. D. begins this short essay by recalling the judgement of the Alexandrian poet Meleager, in 'The Garland', where he weaves into his wreath of Sappho 'few, but roses'. Eileen Gregory discusses the essay in her book *H. D. and Hellenism* (1997), and remarks on the fact that H. D. does not cite the newer fragments of the poet, called the 'Berlin fragments' and known to the poets of her day. H. D. restricts her musings on Sappho to the fragments published by H. T. Wharton in 1885, and although Sappho seems to stand as her predecessor, she approaches her somewhat obliquely. She first takes issue with the Hellenistic Meleager's assessment, calling for not roses, but orange blossoms, 'implacable flowerings made to seduce the sense when every other means has failed, poignard that glints, fresh sharpened steel'. Sappho's words are for her 'colours, or states ... transcending colour yet containing ... all colour'. Then they are rocks, or layers of rock. 'Not flowers at all but an island, a country, a continent, a planet, a world of emotion, differing entirely from any present day imaginable world of emotion'. H. D. invokes an embodied woman, ironic, aristocratic, intolerant, mocking the country girl. 'Her bitterness was on the whole the bitterness of the sweat of Eros' (pp. 57–9).

H. D.'s Sappho is not the worshipper of the Olympian gods, but the petulant, nervous Sappho, lashing out at her companions. She stands in the wind from Asia, in a western gale. H. D. admires her poetic craft, sees her 'artistic wisdom', but questions her emotional, personal wisdom, finding immoderation and inconstancy in love in her poetry. She had 'the wisdom of simplicity, the blindness of genius'. H. D. calls up her child, Cleis, and her beloved girls, made vivid through H. D.'s prose (pp. 65–6):

> angry Eranna who refused everyone and bound white violets only for the straight hair she herself braided with precision and cruel self-torturing neatness about her own head. We know of Gorgo, over-riotous, too heavy, with special intoxicating sweetness, but exhausting, a girl to weary of, no companion, her over-soft curves presaging early development of heavy womanhood.

H. D. is there, on Lesbos, with these women, imagining them fully, projecting from the few words of Sappho's fragment a dense, corporeal reality for these names. She cites the living and the dead, and ends with 'Rhodope', the beauty married by Sappho's brother. So H. D. returns to 'roses', to the rosy-faced 'Graeco-Egyptian beauty' of Naucratis. In the end, she turns back on her rejection of Meleager's characterisation of his predecessor, writing: 'Little – not little – but all, all roses!' She is the 'pseudonym for poignant human feeling', 'rocks set in a blue sea ... the sea itself, breaking and tortured and torturing, but never broken' (p. 67). H. D. remembers all those ancient writers who read her, admired her wisdom – Plato, Meleager, the tragic poet Sophocles, the 'Roman Emperor' who saw life as worth living if he could hear Sappho's songs, Catullus, until the Vatican saw her as a rival to their own 'Poet', and destroyed her poems. She imagines, finally, scholars, hectic antiquaries, searching for 'a precious ... palimpsest among the funereal glories of the sand-strewn Pharaohs' (p. 69). H. D.'s own epitaph, inscribed on her grave in the family plot in Pennsylvania, reveals her debt to Sappho:

> So you may say,
> Greek flower; Greek ecstasy
> reclaims forever
> one who died
> following intricate song's
> lost measure.

H. D. may have lacked the ecstatic identification with the ancient Lesbian poet that some feminists, lesbians and women poets felt, but her poetics, her sense of Sappho as tortured, ironic and not broken, persist in her verse and prose.

The American feminist and lesbian poet Judy Grahn published a set of essays called *The Highest Apple*, in 1985, invoking Sappho in her title. Part III of this text is entitled 'To surface with Lesbian gods'. She lists the many gods of Sappho's world, and continually refers to her present as she reads Sappho's fragments (p. 93):

> Perhaps, in fact, when Sappho speaks of the reddening sweet-apple at the topmost bough, the one that the apple-pickers could not reach – she is singing a womanly song of special protection for the essential female powers; they will never, quite, be reached, and taken from us.

Grahn writes of the lost old gods, and 'their possible reclamation in our modern Lesbian poetry'. She sees Lesbian feminism and its female culture as 'straining to recoup its highest apple'. She reads the work of Emily Dickinson in this light: 'her own love was primarily for women' (pp. 93–4). Amy Lowell, another American poet, is judged as not preoccupying herself 'except indirectly with the re-establishment of the lost female godhead' (p. 100). But H. D. wrote the poem 'Amaranth', which for Grahn 'speaks in Sappho's voice directly to Aphrodite' (p. 194). Audre Lorde reconnects with African divinities, African Amazon figures; Adrienne Rich names 'the forces, the female godforces, and takes as her major subjects love and beauty, intelligence and memory – surely Aphrodite or perhaps the Hebrew Asherah – in another form' (p. 116). Paula Gunn Allen draws on the traditions of indigenous

American female creator gods. Grahn ends her essay on the power of female divinities to inspire her contemporaries, with a return to Sappho and her gods, and she cites in full David Campbell's 1982 prose version of Sappho's first poem: 'Ornate-throned immortal Aphrodite ...' 'Perhaps we are closer to recovering large portions of Sappho's world than we realise' (p. 136).

The influence of Sappho on twentieth-century women's writing extended beyond the Anglophone world. Alejandra Pizarnik, born in Argentina in 1936, lived in exile in Paris and committed suicide in 1972. Her work explores eroticism, ecstasy and depression, and her verses echo some of Sappho's themes, her forms of same-sex desire and the fragmentary form in which we must read her poems. For example:

> Lovers
> a flower
> not far from the night
> my mute body
> opens
> to the delicate urgency of dew

or the poem translated as 'Dawn':

> Nude dreaming a solar night.
> I have lain down animal days.
> The wind and rain erased me
> like a flame, like a poem
> written on a wall.

These beautiful, anguished, sapphic poems, difficult to find in English, were translated by Frank Graziano, Maria Rosa Fort and Suzanne Levine.

Cristina Peri Rossi, a Uruguayan writer born in 1941, was also exiled, and lives in Spain. Her novel *Ship of Fools* satirises dictatorships, embraces feminism and addresses pederasty. The book *Evohé: poemas eróticos*, published in Montevideo in 1971, takes its title, as she says, from 'the onomatopoeic cry of the bacchantes during the feasts and rites paying homage to Bacchus, the god of revelry and wine'. She uses the term, however, as 'an amorous cry: the book proclaims love between two as a form of the Absolute as opposed to the orgy of multiple partners'. She also notes that when first published, *Evohé* 'provoked a considerable scandal. Conditions at the time – just before the military dictatorship – were not favourable to poetry or to erotica. Later, EVOHE was banned entirely, along with the rest of my books'. Peri Rossi sets a fragment of Sappho as the epigrammatic prelude to her book: 'Once again Eros, loosener of limbs, tortures me, sweet and bitter, invincible creature' (pp. 7–9). These poems of Peri Rossi were translated by Diana P. Decker:

> *Dedication I*
> I wrote her many poems
> in fact, I even suffered a little for her.
> I saw her the other day eating in a café
> and the man with her
> kept throwing breadcrumbs in her face.
> I'll publish the poems any day now.
>
> (*Evohé*, p. 15)

> I entered as if into a cathedral
> and her legs vibrated
> like the organ pipes
> when, inside her,
> I began to pronounce her,
> to make music between the naves
> under the acquiescent gaze
> of all the illuminated virgins.
>
> (*Evohé*, p. 97)

Marked by humour, defiance and lesbian eros, Peri Rossi's verses constitute a brilliant, bravado 'translation' of Sappho into another world.

A translation, an understanding, a version of the ancient archaic Lesbian poet Sappho appeared also in some operas that are no longer often performed, including Giovanni Pacini's *Saffo* and Charles Gounod's *Sapho*, both composed in the middle of the nineteenth century. The bel canto *Saffo* of Pacini can be heard in its entirety on YouTube, sung by the great Catalan soprano Montserrat Caballé, who performed the role at the age of 54 in 1987, in her home city of Barcelona. The opera is based on a play by Franz Grillparzer, and depicts Saffo/Sappho at the poetry contest of the 42nd Olympiad at the end of the seventh century BCE. She sings denouncing the tradition of throwing criminals from the Leucadian cliff with the expectation that the god Apollo will rescue them before they die in the sea. Her song is so persuasive that the listeners exile Apollo's high priest, named Alcandro. He swears to take his vengeance on Saffo, and persuades her jealous lover, Faone, that is, Phaon, that she prefers 'Alceo', her fellow Lesbian poet Alkaios. Faone denounces Saffo for her supposed infidelity. Saffo then bonds with the priest's daughter, Climene, agreeing to perform at the latter's wedding, but when she discovers that Climene is to marry Faone, she goes wild, runs amok in song, attempts to stop the wedding and destroys the altar of Apollo. In punishment for her excesses, she herself is exiled. She arrives at the Leucadian cliff, believing that the god Apollo has stricken her with an accursed love for Faone. Planning to throw herself from the white rock, she announces her intentions to jump to the guardian of the cliff, hoping that Apollo will break her fall, rescue her from death and remove the agonising yearning she has for Faone. The guardian, Iphias, agrees to allow her to jump. But an old man in the vicinity overhears their conversation and in a moment of what Aristotle called tragic *peripeteia*, 'reversal', like that in Sophocles' *Oedipus Rex*, he recognises that Saffo is the long-lost daughter of the priest Alcandro. Saffo, her father Alcandro, and Climene her sister have a scene of reconciliation. But Saffo is reminded that she has given a promise to Apollo. She sings a glorious farewell to the assembled group, and jumps. Her sister loses consciousness; Faone wants to jump, but is held back. The god Apollo, unforgiving, lets Saffo drown.

After the decline of the use of *castrati*, male singers whose voices never changed because of surgical castration, women singers came to these roles in the works of Rossini, Donizetti and Bellini, and in the less familiar work of Pacini. This Sappho, like other heroines of bel canto operas, is a tragic, doomed figure. *La sonnambula*, *The Sleepwalker*, by Bellini, first performed in 1831, has the potential for 'coloratura' soprano improvisation; Donizetti's *Lucia di Lammermoor*, of 1835, contains a famous 'mad' scene in which the heroine loses her mind on stage. Some sopranos still perform the aria with the ornate embellishments, not registered in the written score, of the nineteenth century. The composers of bel canto planned their operas allowing for improvisation by the brilliant sopranos of their day, who spontaneously or not elaborated cadenzas, runs, trills, in the margins of the shared musical score, with the orchestra playing forcefully against the arias of the heroines. Although the bel canto style was replaced in the nineteenth century, in the performance of operas by Wagner and by Verdi, some still value the extravagance of these operas and relish the skill of singers who can deploy the high notes and ravishing cadenzas of the tradition. Pacini's *Saffo* allows for all the drama and mad excess of its Romantic, bel canto predecessors.

Charles Gounod's first opera was a *Sapho*, presented somewhat later, in 1851. He had a more respectful stance towards the classical tradition; the Russian author Turgenev wrote of him in a letter:

> His music is like a temple: it is not open to all. I also believe that from his first appearance he will have enthusiastic admirers and great prestige as a musician with the general public; but fickle popularity, of the sort that stirs and leaps like a Bacchante, will never throw its arms around his neck.

Gounod's Sapho is still enamoured of Phaon, but there is also a revolutionary plot, and a rivalry between Sapho and the courtesan Glycère for his affections. The revolutionaries, with Phaon and Glycère, plan to leave their homeland; Sapho in the end again commits suicide by drowning herself in the sea. Phaon will live to see the dawn; she will rest forever under the waves. Her melancholy aria, 'O ma lyre immortelle', 'Oh, my immortal lyre', has survived better than the opera itself. Although Gounod's *Sapho* does not have the extravagance of bel canto arias, this address to her lyre has moved many singers, who seem to identify with this female poet, this singer from antiquity, and her musical instrument, like their prized voices fragile yet immortal.

Twentieth-century musicians kept the name of Sappho alive, although no longer insisting on the legend of the tragic lover of Phaon. Granville Bantock, a British composer, wrote a song cycle for mezzo-soprano and orchestra, between 1900 and 1907, entitled *Sappho*; among the songs, heavily influenced by Richard Wagner, are 'Muse of the Golden Throne' and 'Peer of the Gods He Seems'. The songs, which may have originally been composed for a contralto, and are preceded by an orchestral prelude, were translated by Bantock's wife, Helen Bantock, née Helena von Schweitzer. Bantock's works also include 'Sapphic Poem', for cello and orchestra. The Finnish composer Esa-Pekka Salonen wrote a composition entitled *Five Images after Sappho*, including 'Tell Everyone', 'Without Warning', 'It's No Use', 'The Evening Star' and 'Wedding'. First performed in 1999, the songs are sung by a soprano. Salonen, interestingly enough, while he does not depict the suicidal Sappho, lover of Phaon, nonetheless depicts a heterosexual poet. He wrote about this piece:

> It is the fragmentary nature of the material, and therefore an almost open form, that makes *Sappho* so fascinating to set to music. (After having typed this sentence I realised that I am still trying to give an intellectual, formal explanation wildly off the mark in the good old serialist tradition. That is exactly what I mean by being a prisoner of one's own generation.) It is the tremendous energy of suffocated sexuality and the vibrant eroticism in *Sappho* that got my imagination going. *Sappho* reveals to us secrets of the female soul like nobody else. There is no subject more interesting. Between these small islands of words one can hear music. I set out to compose a cycle in which I would describe a woman's life from childhood to old age and death. Timing was not right: my son Oliver was born in the middle of the composition period, and it became totally impossible for me to imagine death and loneliness. I decided to concentrate on the first part of life instead.
>
> A short description of the structure of *Five Images After Sappho*:
> 1. Tell everyone. The singer explains that she is going to tell a story. Music is fanfare-like, except for the word 'beautifully'.
> 2. Without Warning. The first awakening of love. Descending figures in the beginning are metaphors of a gentle whirlwind.
> 3. It's no use. A young girl is unable to concentrate on household chores. She is trying to explain to her mother why, but gets so

> excited that she can only stutter. Finally, she manages to get the words 'that boy'.
>
> 4. The evening star. I imagine: a girl is lying in the grass in the evening, gazing at the stars. For the first time she understands that even she will be old one day. The strings and the celesta describe the flicker of the stars.
>
> 5. Wedding. I combined several poems here to create a larger form. The singer has different roles in this song. In the refrain the crowd greets the bridegroom. It returns twice in different guises. After the interlude the bride has a brief moment of despair, but is comforted by an older woman ('listen, my dear'), who has a very balanced point of view, in my opinion.
>
> After the second refrain girls gather outside the nuptial chamber and sing teasingly a song ('Come bride').
>
> After the third refrain and an orchestral culmination, a voice describes the couple sleeping peacefully in each other's arms.
>
> (esapekkasalonen.com; http://www.esapekkasalonen.com/compositions/five-images-after-sappho)

Salonen, giving immense power to the singer's voice, is captivated by the 'normative', perhaps imposed, conventional love story of the twentieth century, and disregards the homoerotic content of many of Sappho's fragments.

In the next chapter, 'Queer Sappho', I will consider more fully the ways in which the figure of Sappho enabled the developments in the later twentieth century and the beginnings of the twenty-first of forms of 'homosexual', then 'queer' identity, in the works of feminist writers and queer theorists. But one last example of the 'translated' Sappho, the figure of the poet herself, imagined to be a person, knowable somehow, like twentieth- or twenty-first-century readers, is the entertaining historical novel *The Laughter of Aphrodite*, subtitled *A Novel about Sappho of Lesbos*, by the eminent classicist Peter Green. First published in 1965, the novel was reissued by the University of California Press in 1993. Known for such scholarly and academic historical works as *Alexander to Actium: The Historical Evolution of the Hellenistic Age* (1990), Green follows in the tradition of novelists imagining the life of the poet, from the seventeenth century to the twentieth. Dedicated to William Golding (1911–93), best known as author of *Lord of the Flies*, *The Laughter of Aphrodite* is told in the first-person singular, in the voice of Sappho. The text begins at the end of Sappho's life, and records the sights and smells and bodily sensations of Sappho in Mytilene, citing here and there fragments from the poet's verses: 'my own remembered words mock my helplessness' (p. 2). She is 49 years old, desperately in love with Phaon, who has been bribed by her brother to leave Lesbos. Her memoir, set in a present, moves between her memories of childhood, adolescence, exile and return. She visits Corinth, meets its tyrant, Periander, the famous poet Arion, as well as all the other important historical figures of her day. The form of the novel is that of a *Bildungsroman*, a story of the coming of age, and is here also a story of 'coming out' in the contemporary sense, a novel about the discovery of a disposition towards same-sex eros. Alcaeus is a friend, critical but persistent, and a rival. This Sappho is bisexual; she satisfies her sexual yearnings with her slave girl even as she longs for Phaon, but her desire for her adolescent companions is couched in terms of girlhood 'crushes' that become love.

The novel is marked by Green's residence in Greece, and the worship of Aphrodite that is introduced resembles that of a country church dedicated to the virgin Mary: the choir sings 'Queen of heaven,/ Mother and Virgin', etc. (p. 77). Green imagines the occasion of the composition of various poems; fragment 105a, about the 'highest apple', comes to the adolescent Sappho as she visits a friend's farmhouse (p. 95):

> Suddenly I see, glowing in the last rays of the sun, one perfect, burnished apple, hung in a cluster of dark leaves from the very highest branch. Inexplicable happiness surges up inside me. Perhaps they forgot it? No, I tell myself, with a glance at those broad, purposeful, retreating backs; no, they wouldn't forget. It's the one they couldn't reach, that no one can reach.

There are more pedestrian moments: the poet's mother addresses her sharply: 'Really, Sappho, poetry is no excuse for peevishness.' Sappho marries the wise and tolerant Cercylas in Sicily, and he negotiates their return to Lesbos. She falls in love with Atthis and becomes the leader of a group of friends, all 'girls', 'with artistic interests', which Cercylas names 'the house of the Muses'. There are rival groups. But parents send their daughters from throughout the Aegean to learn literature and the arts from Sappho (p. 217): 'famous director of a highly exclusive finishing school for girls of good family'; rather than seeing this role as incompatible with passionate erotic attachments, Green offers an account of the house of the Muses where for his character Sappho 'the very foundation-stone ... was the love which Atthis and I bore one another—that bright transfiguring passion', although at this stage of the novel that love had not yet been physically consummated. Green portrays Sappho's two brothers, Larichus the beautiful young man, cup-bearer at symposia, and Charaxus, a crude proto-capitalist. The most recently discovered 'new' poem of Sappho, to be considered later in this chapter, expands on the few elements of the lives of these siblings that were previously transmitted in tiny fragments, and in reports of Sappho's biography from long after her life.

In Green's imagination of her life, Sappho's husband Cercylas is killed in the course of the assassination of the tyrant Myrsilus and Pittacus takes power; the aristocrats' coup failed, but Pittacus eventually cedes to a democratically elected council. Sappho is pregnant by Cercylas, 'a seed-pod, a cockpit for explosive natural forces'. She consummates her love with Atthis, but turns against her, brought by Aphrodite to the realisation that blind desire does not last. And Anactoria arrives from Sardis to join the house of the Muses. Sappho's daughter Cleis is born. Sappho later breaks with her grown child, when the mother steals the young man Hippias from her daughter. Atthis speaks the words of fragment 94: 'I'm leaving you', and Sappho responds: 'Honestly, I wish I was dead' (pp. 247–8). In the present moment, recalling these sufferings and yearning for the absent Phaon, she decides to return to Sicily. He had been given a gift by the goddess Aphrodite, in disguise: 'a salve to bring you your heart's desire, Phaon, youth and beauty, the love of women' (p. 253). Sappho's passion for the boatman may have been inflicted by the magic of the goddess. This Sappho is ill and ageing, and must give up her dancing and her house of the Muses; on a convalescent trip with her brother Charaxus, he falls into a passion for the slave girl Doricha who, in Egypt, will ruin him. Sappho attacks him and her rivals, Andromeda, Gorgo and the others. Sailing to Sicily, Sappho passes under the cliffs of Leukas, hears the name of Phaon, killed by a cuckolded husband. She decides to 'make an offering to Apollo' (p. 265) to finish her journey, and asks Poseidon, god of the sea, to 'grant her a gentle passing'. The last words of the fiction are Sappho's fragment 147 in Greek: 'Someone, I say, will afterwards remember us.'

Green ends his book with a short section, 'On Sappho', which explains that he has attempted 'to recreate a famous historical character as faithfully as the evidence at our disposal will allow'. But, because of the mutilated and fragmentary state of that evidence, 'much invention has been necessary'. The novel gives the reader an intense sense of everyday life on Lesbos, and this is its most powerful aspect. He writes from Methymna, on the island of Lesbos, which he cites as a source of evidence for his inspiration: 'a "rosy-fingered moon" after sunset will come as no surprise to an islander' (pp. 267–8). Once again, as in the case of Ovid, and of John Donne, a man takes pleasure in inhabiting the consciousness of a woman, a woman in Green's case who has turned from the love of girls to the desire for an (absent) man. This literary transvestism continues to have its fascination, and is a compelling part of the history of Sappho, of our understanding of that history.

I want to turn now from the 'translation', the re-inscription, of the person, the character, the figure Sappho, from Ovid's suicidal lover of Phaon and her many descendants, from French novelists, playwrights and poets, Michael Field and Swinburne, the operatic Sapphos, the Sapphos of neoclassical painting, to the history of literary translation, with an emphasis on the rendering into English of Sappho's lyrics as they arrived, buried in the texts of other classical scholars, culled from fragmentary papyri over centuries, up to the most recently discovered of fragments, deciphered in 2014 on a scrap of papyrus from the third century CE, an expanded version of a poem which concerns Sappho's brothers.

Translations of poetry, of necessity, vary greatly with mutations in poetic conventions through generations, and with individual, private reactions from translators. A telling example of transformations in translations of Sappho is revealed, as Yopie Prins has noted, in tracking the many centuries of her fragment 31, which was transmitted safely embedded in the text of the writer conventionally called 'Longinus', author of *On the Sublime*, who probably lived in the first century CE. In the post-medieval period his text was not published until the sixteenth century, and, as noted earlier, was translated by the Frenchman Nicolas Boileau in the seventeenth century. Centuries earlier the poem had been translated into Latin by the Roman poet Catullus, as I described in the previous chapter; Catullus positioned himself within the imaginary scene of a woman falling apart as she watches her beloved. For Catullus, translating Sappho provided the opportunity to describe a man distraught at seeing his beloved with another man, and he translated the crucial, and difficult, Greek line *alla kam men glossa [m'] eage* (in Daley's translation 'for my tongue cracks') as *lingua sed torpet*, 'but my tongue is numb' (poem 51).

Sappho's poem found many translators in the centuries after Catullus' version, not only because of its accessibility and seeming completeness, but also because of the intensity of its depiction of anguished desire. Ronsard translated it, and Racine, as noted earlier, embedded allusion to it in his tragedy *Phèdre*. In English, in the sixteenth-century poet Sir Philip Sidney's romance, *The Countess of Pembroke's Arcadia*, published in 1593, after the death of the author, the editors embedded reference to Sappho's fragment 31 in the form of one of its 'eclogues'. The proto-novel, or heroic romance, takes place in a pastoral setting, indebted to Anyte, Theokritos, Virgil and all the intervening writers who repopulate the world of Arcadia with shepherds and shepherdesses who have extraordinary poetic powers and engage in erotic and poetic rivalries. Sidney's *Arcadia*, like Shakespearean comedies, teems with cross-dressing, transvestism and confusion of the sexes. In the printed version of the *New Arcadia*, at a certain point in the extremely convoluted plot, which combines pastoral with a dramatic narrative, one of the characters, the disguised Amazon Zelmane, begins to sing 'in Anacreon's kind of verses', although in fact the words echo those of Sappho's fragment:

> My muse, what ails this ardour?
> Mine eyes be dim, my limbs shake,
> My voice is hoarse, my throat scorched,
> My tongue to this my roof cleaves,

> My fancy amazed, my thoughts dulled,
> My heart doth ache, my life faints,
> My soul begins to take leave:
> So great a passion all feel
> To think a sore so deadly
> I should so rashly rip up.
>
> (*The Countess of Pembroke's Arcadia*, Book 2, 'Second Eclogues')

The symptoms of love, transmitted from Sappho through centuries of literary imitation and adaptation, have become canonical, even comical in some contexts. The blazon, derived from the verses of the Tuscan poet Petrarch, catalogued the beauties of the beloved woman's body, one by one, from head to toe, and also became part of the vocabulary of erotic verse throughout Western lyric. But Sappho's erotic self-examination, her portrait of her own body falling to pieces, nearing death, as she gazed towards her beloved, offers another paradigm of erotic possession, looking outwards but feeling inwardly the effects of desire, in contrast to the Petrarchan lover's focus on the other.

The translations of Sappho's fragment 31, whether free-standing, as Sappho's verses, or incorporated into other texts, as in Sidney's *Arcadia*, included the eighteenth-century John Addison's 'Whilst I gaz'd, my Voice was lost'. Lord Byron, who died in the cause of independence for Greece from the Ottoman Empire, wrote of the ancient poets in *Don Juan*:

> Oh, Love! of whom great Caesar was the suitor,
> Titus the master, Antony the slave,
> Horace, Catullus, scholars, Ovid tutor,
> Sappho the sage blue-stocking, in whose grave
> All those may leap who rather would be neuter –
> (Leucadia's rock still overlooks the wave) –
> Oh, Love! thou art the very god of evil,
> For, after all, we cannot call thee devil.
>
> (*Don Juan*, Canto II, 205)

Here Byron wittily alludes to Sappho's reputation as the chaste schoolmistress, a learned 'blue-stocking', but then also to her supposed bisexuality, among those 'who rather would be neuter', and posits that her neuter desire projected her over the rock of Leukas. Elsewhere, in Canto III, 83 of *Don Juan*, Byron salutes Greece, still under the domination of the Ottomans, and again invokes Sappho: 'The isles of Greece! the isles of Greece!/ Where burning Sappho loved and sung ... Eternal summer gilds them yet,/ But all, except their sun, is set.' And Byron also alluded to Sappho's fragment 31 in his description of bodily suffering: 'Parch'd to the throat my tongue adheres.' The line is echoed by Tennyson, by John Addington Symonds, poet of 'male love', and by T. H. Rearden: 'When I but saw you, from my gasping throat, nor speech nor sound issued; Then my tongue brake falt'ring.' These earlier translations used end-rhymes, and often sought to conform Sappho's verse to the conventions of English poetry, including its traditional metres based on stress rather than on syllable length, which was the practice in ancient Greek and Latin. In the ancient languages, a vowel like *omega*, that is, the 'big o', was understood to take longer to pronounce than *omicron*, that is, 'little o'. Although there were attempts to replicate such a metrical practice, as in early seventeenth-century poetry, where Thomas Campion wrote, 'Rose-cheek'd Laura, come', imitating the long and short syllables of ancient verse, the stress metres of English became the norm.

Twentieth-century translators, with an eye to modernist aesthetic principles, no longer sought to make Sappho's lines rhyme, nor to imitate her metres. Ezra Pound was moved by the recent discovery of fragments of Sappho's work unearthed in Egypt and by Richard Aldington's translation of Sappho's fragment 96 as 'To Atthis', published in 1914. Pound wrote his own fragmentary allusion to the Lesbian poet:

> *Papyrus*
> Spring......
> Too long......
> Gongula......

Basil Bunting, in 1927, translated Sappho's line 'my tongue thickens, my ears ring'. In 1958 the great American poet William Carlos Williams, with admirable simplicity, rendered it:

> At mere sight of you
> my voice falters, my tongue
> Is broken.

The slim volume of Mary Barnard, published by the University of California Press also in 1958, had a profound impact on lovers of poetry, classical scholars and translators, incorporating as it did the aesthetic ideals of the modernists, including Ezra Pound. Barnard wrote:

> If I meet
> you suddenly, I can't
> speak – my tongue is broken.

Barnard's translations have been criticised for the liberties she took with the Greek text of such fragments; yet her translations sat beautifully, like haikus on the page, using the white space surrounding them to emphasise a spare, fragmentary beauty. And her translations remain profoundly influential. The classicist Richmond Lattimore, who produced unsurpassed translations of Homer's *Iliad* and *Odyssey*, published this version of the line, in 1960: 'Let me only glance where you are, the voice dies, I can say nothing, but my lips are stricken to silence.' 'My tongue sticks to my dry mouth' is the version of Guy Davenport, published in 1980; Diane Rayor gives the reader 'I say nothing, my tongue broken', in her impressive translation of ancient Greek poetry published in 1991. M. L. West, another classicist, very literal in his renderings, translated 'for watching you a moment, speech fails me, my tongue is paralysed'. Translations proliferated in the second half of the twentieth century, in part because of feminist interest in Sappho and because of a new attention to women's history in general. David Campbell (1982) provided the Greek text of Sappho's fragments as well as the *testimonia*, biographical materials and remarks on Sappho preserved in other ancient authors; although not prosaic, his prose translation is: 'my tongue snapped.' Paul Roche (1984), who in the introduction to the first version of his translations, regrettably called Sappho an 'invert' but not a 'pervert', gives us: 'My tongue breaks up.' Willis Barnstone, in *Sappho and the Greek Lyric Poets* (1988), has: 'my voice is empty.' In the twenty-first century the brilliant poet, classicist and translator Anne Carson, who translated all the legible fragments in 2002, in *If Not, Winter*, translated these lines as:

> for when I look at you, even a moment, no speaking
> is left in me
>
> no: tongue breaks ...

Translations of the fragments continue to appear; Diane Rayor has published a volume focused exclusively on Sappho. Penguin will issue, in 2015, a volume in its 'Little Black Classics' series, 80 books, a celebration of 80 years of Penguins, a translation of Sappho called *Come Close*.

Each of the older translations has its virtues and flaws. Mary Barnard's translation, for example, so influential on many readers, unfortunately gives headings to some of the poems, with titles that confusingly merge with the poems themselves, as with fragment 16, which bears the title 'To an army wife, in Sardis', noted in Chapter 2, an implicit interpretation that inappropriately affects the reader's experience of this poem. There is no wife, no army wife, no Sardis, in the poem itself, and Barnard's, or her editors' situating the poem in this way has led it, for example, to be anthologised in a volume on 'women in war', when the burden of the verses seems to focus rather on eros, desire, and the sparkling if imagined presence of the beloved.

In an interview, the poet John Daley discussed the principles that guided his translation of many of Sappho's fragments, published as *Fragments of Sappho*, with my introduction and prints by the artist Julie Mehretu, by Arion Press in 2011. He noted the words of the poet Ezra Pound, that 'Only emotion endures', and 'Nothing matters save the quality of affection.'

Influenced by the work of Robert Creeley, Robert Duncan, Alan Ginsberg, Ed Dorn and Alice Notley, Daley gravitated to Sappho as another poet who presents a range of emotions, 'from joy to sorrow'. John Ashbery too has had his impact on Daley's thinking, a model of liberating verse from the constriction of thought; Ashbery's fragmentary, dispersive style, embedding in a whole poem allusions, thoughts and a wide variety of cultural materials, also appealed to Daley. With regard to Sappho's fragments: 'One can hear them, not need to forge them into coherence, allow for fractures of time.' Reading Ashbery with Sappho, Daley noted that Ashbery calls all art 'surreal'; Sappho's fragments created for him a 'surreal', super-real surface. Yet 'the voice still wants its coherence – it drives toward that – even in language poetry, the language drives toward that'. So Daley, in the deconstruction and reconstruction of Sappho's verses, sensed a person in the words, understood a body behind the Greek. His technique was, in consultation with me, to establish a field of possible English meanings of the Greek, alternatives for any particular phrase, and from that to develop 'a thread of the voice'. The Greek was preserved in the English translation, as a 'base meaning', as syllabic presence in metre, a 'tightness' that was maintained there, almost as a mathematical object. He saw his task as not producing a text 'the same' as Sappho's Greek, not 'rendering it', but rather keeping 'the count' as close as possible to the Greek metres, without insisting on replication of the stresses, the rhythmic shape of the fragments in Greek. He said at one point in the interview, echoing Flaubert: 'I am Sappho; I hope she doesn't mind.'

Greek, like Latin, marks the relationship of words not by placement in the sentence, 'Atthis sees Gongyla', where the object of the verb follows the verb, but rather resembles 'You see me', where 'me' is in the so-called 'accusative' case, different from 'I' when it is the object of the verb. Sappho, like all ancient poets, writes with the fluidity afforded by these possibilities of language, juxtaposing words that in English have to be separated for the syntax, the word order of a sentence, to work. For example, where the word 'golden' occurs in fragment 1, the word in Greek could refer either to the 'house' of Zeus, or to the 'chariot' of Aphrodite. Daley in his translation registers this ambiguity by hanging the word 'golden' between the stanzas of the poem. And we have attempted to render Sappho's language, without falling into various traps to which translators can be susceptible. Sappho's language is, in our view, sometimes intimate, but rarely casual, colloquial or idiomatic. Daley has preserved the sometimes ceremonial formality of some poems, the tender intimacy of others, without imagining that they are necessarily private communications between lovers.

In relation to the modes of punctuation chosen to represent Sappho's fragmentary poems in English, Daley recalled an exhibition he had seen at the Louvre Museum in Paris in 2010, on the Meroe culture of ancient Africa, called 'Empire on the Nile'. Stone tablets on display bore both hieroglyphic and cursive characters, and the sign : : appeared on the texts. This mark inspired the choice of : : to punctuate the fragmentary words of Sappho in his translation. Asked about the new poems that have come to light, only one of which was translated in 2010, Daley said: 'More life out of the ancient world.'

A fuller version of fragment 58, long known in a mutilated form, was published in 2005. I've chosen to discuss this poem here, separately from the consideration of the other fragments in Chapters 1 and 2, to mark the ways in which this unexpected discovery came as a surprise to readers of Sappho, and to take the occasion to think about how this poem, which is written in the voice of an ageing woman, may have changed our view of the poet. This is Daley's translation:

> You children, a beautiful gift from the violet bosomed muses,
> be eager for love's clear voiced song and the tortoiseshell lyre.
>
> But for me old age has now seized my once delicate skin,
> and so white has become my hair once black.
>
> My heart has been made heavy, and my knees won't support me –
> knees, which once were nimble and danced like fawns.
>
> These things I often sigh about, but what can be done?
> For a human being, it's not possible to be ageless.

> Once upon a time, they say, Tithonos was carried away
> in the rose arms of Eos as she by love took him to the ends of earth.
>
> He, so beautiful and young, was nonetheless still overtaken
> in time by old age having a deathless bedmate.
>
> But I love luxury : :   This for me Eros has allotted   :
> the brilliance and beauty of the sun.

There is much to say about this poem, which supplements an earlier fragment also much commented on. The voice of the poet here, as elsewhere, speaks of her regrets about ageing, calling to her young companions to listen to the music of the lyre. She, once agile as a fawn, has been stricken by age. She recalls her former fleetness, and reminds the listener of the myth, the tale, the story of Eos and Tithonos as an exemplum to demonstrate the inevitability of human ageing. The story is familiar from the *Homeric Hymn to Aphrodite* in which, after seducing Anchises, the goddess reminds him of the fate of Eos' mortal lover (lines 217–38):

> So ... , golden-throned Eos abducted Tithonos,
> One of your own race, who resembled the immortals.
> She went to ask Kronion, lord of dark clouds,
> That he should be immortal and live forever.
> And Zeus nodded assent to her and fulfilled her wish.
> Mighty Eos was too foolish to think of asking
> Youth for him and to strip him of baneful old age.
> Indeed, so long as much-coveted youth was his,
> He took his delight in early-born, golden-haired Eos,
> And dwelt by the stream of Okeanos at the ends of the earth.
> But when the first grey hairs began to flow down
> From his comely head and noble chin,
> Mighty Eos did refrain from his bed,
> Though she kept him in her house and pampered him
> With food and ambrosia and gifts of fine clothing.

> But when detested old age weighed heavy on him
> And he could move or lift none of his limbs,
> This is the counsel that to her seemed best in her heart:
> She placed him in a chamber and shut its shining doors.
> His voice flows endlessly and there is no strength,
> Such as there was before, in his crooked limbs.
>
> (Translated by Apostolos Athanassakis)

This sad story returns in the form of the Sibyl alluded to by T. S. Eliot; she too is deathless but not ageless, and her voice cries from inside a bottle: 'I want to die.'

The work of the historian Hellanikos of Lesbos records a further development of the story, as a commentary on the description of the old men of Troy as they watch from their city's battlements and are likened, with their frail, crackling voices, to cicadas (*Iliad* 3.150–2):

> Now through old age these fought no longer, yet were they excellent
> speakers still, and clear, as cicadas through the forest
> settle on trees, to issue their delicate voice of singing.
>
> (Translated by Richmond Lattimore)

A scholiast, an ancient commentator on these lines, reports that Hellanikos says that Tithonos son of Laomedon, brother of Priam, was the beloved of the goddess Day, to whom she bore Memnon. Tithonos having been used up, consumed, spent, Eos turned him into a cicada. And on account of this the poet likens the kinsmen, elders of the city, to cicadas.

Elsewhere in the *Iliad* and *Odyssey*, Eos, or Dawn the rose-fingered, rises from the bed of Tithonos, perhaps a god himself, still in the vigour of his manhood. But the story fits into a pattern that includes Selene and Endymion, Aphrodite and Adonis, Aphrodite and Phaon, as well as other young men taken from the mortal realm by the Dawn goddess. The cicadas sing without sustenance, living on music, as Plato tells us in the *Phaedrus* (259bc):

> The story is that once upon a time these creatures were men – men of an age before there were any Muses – and that when the latter came into the world, and music made its appearance, some of the people of those days were so thrilled with pleasure that they went on singing, and quite forgot to eat and drink until they actually died without noticing it. From them in due course sprang the race of cicadas, to which the Muses have granted the boon of needing no sustenance right from their birth, but of singing from the very first, without food or drink, until the day of their death, after which they go and report to the Muses how they severally are paid honour among mankind, and by whom.
>
> (Translated by R. Hackforth, in *The Collected Dialogues of Plato*)

In Sappho's poem, the love of the goddess has a more sinister aspect, like that recorded in the *Homeric Hymn to Aphrodite*. Rather than a glorious immortality among the Muses, or a position as cup-bearer to Zeus, like Ganymede, Tithonos has his youth sucked from him, and he ends as a voice without a body. This may be a consolation to an ageing poet, who seeks a monument more lasting than bronze, but it suggests a resignation to her loss of the power to invoke the protection of the goddess and a fear of the rosy-armed goddess and her powers. The destructive, consuming mother gives her lover immortality, but allows him to wither, desiccated and almost disembodied, without the moist, juicy attributes of flourishing life. His voice is the remainder, resisting consumption and obliteration, stubbornly persisting, irreducible.

This discovery of this poem had an impact on study of Sappho's fragments. There had been shreds of fragments earlier, lines that alluded to ageing. Fragment 125: 'I wove, used to weave garlands', preceded by a word difficult to decipher, may suggest that once upon a time, in her youth, Sappho wove garlands. Fragment 121, from the ancient author Stobaeus, reads: 'But being my dear one,/ take the bed of someone younger,/ for I will not tolerate living in wedlock, being the elder ...' The fuller version of fragment 58 expands our sense of this poet regretting the loss of agility she once knew, but also accepting the inevitability of death. Tithonos did not die, but his fate was not a happy one. Nonetheless, his voice lived on, like that of a cicada; and perhaps there is a hope expressed that Sappho's own voice, her verses, will survive her. And in any case, luxury, and eros, the light of the sun, have given her life.

Since the publication of Sappho's fragments by Daley, in 2011, more, fuller poems have been discovered on papyri previously unknown to textual scholars. One of the new fragments, called 'The Kypris poem', fills out missing portions of fragment 26, and is addressed to Aphrodite, 'Queen Kypris', the Cyprus-born one. The voice in the poem complains to the goddess about how repeated anguish is the result of yearning to make someone one's own. Most significant, and adding to our sense of Sappho's regret at ageing and the inevitability of death, is the fragment called 'The Brothers poem', which came to light in 2014. Peter Green's novel incorporates some of the traditional knowledge about Sappho's brothers, the younger, Larikhos, a cup-bearer at feasts in Mytilene, the other Kharaxos, known from Herodotos' and others' reports concerning his infatuation with the slave *hetaira* Dorikha, or 'Rhodopis', the rosy-faced. Herodotos says that Sappho 'violently abused' her brother after he freed the woman from slavery. Dorikha is mentioned in Sappho's fragments 7 and 15; a new fragment, found on a papyrus, contains in mutilated form the poem now called 'The Brothers'.

To illustrate the process of how new papyri can change our perception, our understanding, of Sappho, I cite here John Daley's 2011 translation of fragment 5, which concerns the brother of Sappho. The questions marks and the ellipses indicate how the papyrus was in great part illegible; textual editors have tried to read, tried to supplement, or guess from context what might have been there in the missing sections.

> O Kypris and Nereids grant that unharmed
> my brother arrive back here to me.
> And whatever his heart wishes to happen,
>   grant that all this will happen.
>
> And however many times before he missed the mark, let it go,
> and let him become a delight to his loved ones,

and a grief for his enemies. And may there never more be
>   anyone who is a misery to us.

And may he then want his sister to partake in honor,
>   but sore grief ...   ... before in sorrow ...

These are intimate poems, probably not performed chorally on ceremonial occasions, like the wedding songs, without the formality of other more public verse. The Kypris fragment points to the persistence of Sappho's devotion to the goddess Aphrodite and to her resort to prayer to the goddess when she finds herself in distress concerning love. The other new fragment also touches on Sappho's brothers, naming both and thus confirming some of the anecdote in Herodotos about Kharaxos' adventures in Egypt with the slave *hetaira* Dorikha/Rhodopis. This is John Daley's translation of the new lines found in 2014:

> Yet again you babble, 'Kharaxos comes!
> His ship is full!' I think these things are for Zeus
> to know, as do all the gods. No need for you
>   to think about them.
>
> But instead, send me, order me out
> to pray and pray, beg Queen Hera
> so Kharaxos may arrive here
>   guiding his ship
>
> to find us safe and sound. For in these,
> as in all things, let's turn to the gods –
> for calms out of mighty gales
>   may suddenly come.
>
> If the lord of Olympus chooses,
> a god as help comes and turns things around –
> out of troubles, people come to be happy,
>   the richly blessed ones.

> And we, if Larikhos could lift his head
> and ever become a man,
> then we, after so much heavy heartedness,
> suddenly we'd be free.

The voice in the poem addresses someone, speaking colloquially, chattily, about the return of Kharaxos, perhaps from Egypt, from a voyage, with his merchant's ship full of cargo. As noted, the name of Sappho's brother, here seen as arriving with a ship full of trade goods, supports some of the biographical data about Sappho found in historians and others who write much later about her life. The reference to Zeus, and 'all the gods', adds to our growing sense of Sappho as polytheist, devoted not exclusively to Aphrodite as goddess of eros, but also to Zeus, to all these gods, to Hera the queen. And she beseeches Hera again to provide safe passage for those in jeopardy on the sea, in this world in which journeys like those of Kharaxos, threading among the islands, along the western coast of Asia, to Cyprus, Crete and north Africa, built networks of connection, exchange and profit, but also exposed those sailing to the dangers of shipwreck and loss. The poem alludes to the protection of the gods and to the suddenness of changes of fortune, calm and storm, help and trouble, blessings from Zeus and other *daimones*, other gods, who can capriciously, or in return for prayers, alter the fate of those who worship them. From the somewhat scornful first line, mocking the babbler who exclaims at the arrival of Kharaxos, the poem enacts a shift from storm to calm, from a troubled state to happiness. And then, at the last, the poet imagines both an unsatisfactory brother, perhaps, one who was beautiful and served as cup-bearer to the notables of Mytilene, but who droops at present, and needs to grow up. If he were to assume his manhood, then the family, once burdened with the weight of worry and perhaps even financial difficulty, would find themselves in the situation of blessed, wealthy happiness. And there may even be a reference to slavery and freedom here; Kharaxos was said to have bought the freedom of the slave *hetaira* Dorikha/Rhodopis. The last words of this poem are *aipsa lutheimen*, 'suddenly, we are free'. The metaphorical escape from bondage might allude to the great expense incurred by Sappho's brother, in freeing his lover; the family, too, will suddenly be free.

The translations of this newly discovered poem vary dramatically. This last line, in the versions published in the *Times Literary Supplement*, for example, ranges from Anne Carson's 'We'll run our fingers/ through his beard and laugh', to the more sober 'Then what a cargo of cares at once would drop/ From the heart' of A. E. Stallings. Once again, we see how much the individual choices of translators, close to the Greek or veering far, determine the reader's sense of Sappho's voice. As I argued in the Introduction, our understanding of Sappho is mediated, tempered, dependent, altered over many centuries, by the cultural environment in which her fragments are received as well as by the arrival of new fragments, from waste dumps or libraries. There is no stable 'Sappho', no fixed person, no knowable biography, no final set of 'collected works'. Understanding Sappho requires an openness to change, to millennia of change, and to the whole history of readers of this life, these poems.

V

Queer Sappho

I COULD IDENTIFY MANY MOMENTS as the beginning of what has come to be called 'queer theory', or 'queer studies'. The works of the women of Paris in the early part of the twentieth century, members of the 'Sapho 1900' group, would count there, as well as the wave of feminists, among them Luce Irigaray, Hélène Cixous and Monique Wittig, who published crucial texts in the period after May 1968. Monique Wittig's works in particular, mentioned in the previous chapter, included not only an intense concentration on lesbian eros, but also a weaving of the ancient Lesbian poet Sappho into her writing. *Les Guérillères* (1969) lists woman warriors, and Amaterasu, a Japanese sun goddess, and Cihuacoatl, a Mesoamerican goddess, figure in their story. The women celebrate (p. 62):

> Drunk, the women say they are drunk. Great fields of scarlet poppies have been trampled underfoot. Their heads, their torn petals hang loosely or lie in confusion on the ground. Not a drop of dew is visible on the flowers. The women dance. They hold each other round the neck and let themselves fall to the ground, lips black, eyes starting. They say they are drunk. Their arms and legs are bare. Their loosened hair hides their cheeks, then, flung back, reveals shining eyes, lips parted in song.

The woman guerrillas form a choir, like one of those formed of girls participating in ritual in archaic Greece. Until the time of Hippolyta, Queen of the Amazons, women had always been defeated. But these women are prepared for battle: 'They say they have the strength of the lion the hate of the tiger the cunning of the fox the patience of the cat the perseverance of the horse the tenacity of the jackal' (p. 119).

Women's names of all nations are listed between episodes in Wittig's text, among them many Greek names, Chryseis, Diotima, Nausicaa, Anactoria, Psappha. This book had an international readership and contributed to the formation of a feminist and lesbian consciousness in the 1960s and 1970s. The original publication records sources for Wittig's text, including Sappho; for some reason this last word is omitted from the English translation by David Le Vay.

As noted in Chapter 4, Wittig's *Lesbian Peoples: Material for a Dictionary*, published in 1976 with Sande Zeig, contains a blank page headed 'Sappho'. Wittig's *The Lesbian Body* (1973) refers frequently to Sappho; early on, it calls on the ancient Lesbian writer (p. 16):

> At this point *I* invoke your help m/y incomparable Sappho, give m/e by thousands the fingers that allay the wounds, give m/e the lips the tongue the saliva which draw one into the slow sweet poisoned country from which one cannot return.

Wittig inscribes an implicit critique of the personal pronoun in her work; because it assumes a masculine gender, she undoes the writing of 'je', 'j/e' cutting the word in two to emphasise the submerging of the feminine in the masculine, the unquestioned complementarity of woman to man in language. The translator, David Le Vay, solved the problem of the single letter of the English 'I' by italicising it.

In the violence and fusion and undoing of eros, Wittig calls in *The Lesbian Body* to 'dark and gilded Lesbos' (p. 26); 'Sappho has written it for eternity that Latone and Niobe love each other with a tender love' (p. 31). 'You are m/yself (aid m/e Sappho) you are m/yself ...' (p. 50). Again and again in this text she summons the archaic Lesbian poet: 'm/y mouth opens to entreat the divine incomparable Sappho'; 'glory to Sappho for as long as we shall live in this dark continent' (p. 57). Like many other readers of the fragments over the centuries, Wittig records an erotic disintegration: 'the intensity is too great, *I* feel *I* cannot stand it, *I* faint away, but not before m/y saphenous nerves are touched, who would have believed it m/y Sappho' (p. 61). As the women dance, the voice of the author picks out 'Sappho of the violet breasts', (p. 69), 'Sappho the golden' (p. 70). She worships Ishtar-Astarte (p. 93), prays to Sappho (p. 97), walks over the 'black earth' (p. 113): 'Sappho when I beseech her causes a violet lilac-smelling rain to fall over the island.' The voice in the text says: '*I* stand erect, mouth open, *I* thank Sappho the very tender goddess while you m/y very radiant one hold m/y hands' (p. 114). Sappho has been divinised; she is a goddess like the ancient Mesopotamian Ishtar. As the author admires her lover, she praises 'Sappho the all-attentive', and explores the body of the beloved: '*I* inhale you m/y very odoriferous one, you smell very headily of lilac, Sappho could have done no better by clasping you against her violet breasts, now *I* lick you'; 'glory to Sappho over centuries of centuries' (p. 116). In the violence, the fusion of lovers, the voice of the text speaks of wrenching out the teeth of the other, and offering them to 'Sappho the most distant' (p. 127). The author glories in her own goddess-hood, writing: '*I* am seated in the highest of the heavens in the starry circle where dwells Sappho of the violet cheeks, as with her the stars' dazzle pales m/y cheeks, *I* am the sovereign one.' Throughout this great vision, a delirious, hallucinatory passage, Sappho is there, among all the other great and powerful females of history, presiding over a community of women, loving, devouring, being devoured, seeking one another. Wittig seems to erase the distinction some have made, between 'Lesbian', an adjective referring to the island of Lesbos, and thus to Sappho, but also to Alkaios, to everything connected with this Aegean island, and 'lesbian', that is, referring to women whose erotic desire is focused on other women. For Wittig, Sappho the Lesbian is a lesbian, an ancestress, a goddess.

The 'French feminism' of generations following in the path of 'Sapho 1900', and subsequent to the revolutionary movements of 1968, came with women's liberation, civil rights struggles in the US, resistance to the war in Vietnam and also agitation for gay rights. Sappho figured in these movements; for example, the artist Judy Chicago, in her work *The Dinner Party* (1974–9), set a place at her table for Sappho, a plate depicting a flowering, open vagina with labia. In the US, after the Stonewall riots of 1969, attention to the oppression of gay people became a burning issue. With the arrival of HIV/AIDS, and the government's failure to respond to its devastating effects on gay communities in the US, groups like ACT UP emerged, ever more militant, with chants such as 'We're here, we're queer, get used to it.' The use of the word 'queer', once a pejorative term used to dismiss gay men, became a badge of honour, and came to define not just gay, not just lesbian, but also other forms of 'non-heteronormative' persons, that is, transgender, transsexual, transvestite, bisexual, intersex, sex workers and any other variety of proud deviance from what was once called 'compulsory heterosexuality'.

Another aspect of this history is the pioneering work of the French philosopher and historian Michel Foucault. His *History of Sexuality*, vol. 1, *An Introduction*, published in Paris in 1976 as *La Volonté de savoir*, had a huge impact not only on academic work, but also on sexual politics. Having written earlier on the history of medicine, of madness, of punishment, Foucault had envisioned the history of sexuality as a seven-volume series. This first volume sought to undermine what he called 'the repressive hypothesis', the notion that Victorian, nineteenth- and early twentieth-century society repressed the topic of sexuality, insisting rather that the diffuse power of medicine and psychoanalysis required speech about sexuality, was an incitement to discuss and analyse sexual life, that the 'talking cure' of psychoanalysis replaced the Catholic confessional as a way of managing and governing bodies. In the second and third volumes of the *History of Sexuality* Foucault changed direction, and went back to the ancient Greek and Roman worlds to delineate the development of techniques of mastering and caring for the self that gave the lie to those who claimed Christianity as the cause of increasing chastity, celibacy and companionate marriage in the early centuries of the common era. His book on the ancient Greeks, *The Use of Pleasures*, *L'Usage des plaisirs* (1984), discusses principally prescriptive classical Greek texts, with little mention of the erotic practices of the archaic age and the magnificent lyric poetry of that period. And there is nothing about Sappho, or eros between women. Ancient Athenian 'wives', like boys, present occasions for mastery and self-mastery by the philosophical male subject.

Classical scholarship on sexuality, building on an interest in women's lives spurred in part by the feminist movements of the twentieth century, flowered before the publication of Foucault's work, but further in response to it. Passionate debates arose concerning Foucault's claims concerning the nature of ancient sexuality. Were there 'homosexuals' in ancient Greece and Rome? Was there homophobia in ancient Greece and Rome? Scholars sought evidence in various sources. The comic poet Aristophanes of the fifth century BCE seems to disapprove of same-sex love, or at least of mature men continuing to assume the position of 'the penetrated' in anal intercourse. The Romans used pejorative language, adopted from Greek, to describe so-called 'passive partners' in male same-sex eros, and the satirist Juvenal wrote disparagingly of women exhibiting masculine, gladiatorial tendencies.

The writer Plutarch, a Greek who became a Roman, wrote in the first or second century CE not only his famed *Lives* but also a 'Dialogue on Love', now collected in the *Moralia*, an eclectic set of essays and speeches. This fragmentary 'dialogue', really a monologue by Plutarch's son Autoboulus, recalls the words of Plutarch himself in a debate that took place years before at a sanctuary of the Muses in Greece. In the town below Mount Helikon, sacred to the Muses, during a celebration of Eros, a rich widow seeks to marry a beautiful younger man; friends debate the matter of love. One of those arguing concedes that there may be pleasure in intercourse between a man and a woman, but it is 'an effeminate and bastard love' (750f). For him, 'there is only one genuine Love, the love of boys' (751a). A lively debate ensues about conjugal love, marriage, eros between men and women, and the power of love, for example the same-sex love of men producing heroism on the battlefield: 'lover and beloved, when their god is present, no enemy has ever encountered and forced his way through' (761c). The speaker, in his defence of love, even cites Sappho herself: 'Sappho speaks words mingled truly with fire; through her song she communicates the heat of her heart.' He asks one of those present to recite her fragment 31, in which 'the fair Sappho describes how her voice is lost and her body burns; how she turns pale, reels, and grows giddy when her beloved appears' (763a). He uses the feminine form of the word 'beloved', *eromenes*. The speaker Plutarch, having heard the verses, calls this 'divine possession', following Plato's description of erotic madness. The god Eros oversees all these forms of desire, but especially that of same-sex lovers. The true lover is excited by beauty, and brought to a celebration of the god's mysteries. Love must not be forced, but it accompanies a philosophical life. Plutarch ends with a celebration of conjugal union and affection, saying that physical union is the beginning of friendship between husband and wife. He praises Solon, the Athenian lawgiver of the sixth century BCE, who enforced conjugal intercourse by law (769a):

> Solon was a very experienced legislator of marriage laws. He prescribed that a man should consort with his wife not less than three times a month – not for pleasure, surely, but as cities renew their mutual agreements from time to time.

The 'dialogue' ends with the marriage of the young widow and the beautiful boy. Plutarch's views seem to herald a changing attitude towards marriage between a man and a woman, which is advised in other philosophical and medical writings.

Yet the greatest poets, and most honoured philosophers, Plato, Horace, Virgil and of course Sappho, expressed passionate attachment for lovers of their own gender, and the recognition of the power of same-sex attraction, and the value of such eros, persists throughout Greek and Roman antiquity. In the text entitled *Erotes*, that is *Amores*, translated as *Affairs of the Heart*, attributed falsely to the second-century CE author Lucian, the author, probably writing in the early fourth century CE, bears witness to the *persistence* of homoeroticism, same-sex love between men and between women, in ancient Greek and Roman culture. In a dialogue between two characters, Lycinus asks his friend Theomnestus to tell him of his love affairs, 'with a lad or even with a girl'. Theomnestus is a victim of Aphrodite, and he pounces on any and every beauty who passes; he has been smitten by love for both boys and women. His partner in conversation, Lycinus, seems indifferent to both sorts of love, although he reminisces about the oddity of two men, one who took delight only in boys, the other in women. Such exclusive preferences are remarkable in the world in which the dialogue takes place, and Lycinus recalls in detail their defence of their particular tastes. The first, Charicles of Corinth, 'showed some evidence of the skilful use of cosmetics'. Lycinus interprets this as a sign of his desire to attract women. The other man, Callicratidas, was a manly Athenian, a devotee of physical training who loved only boys. The ancient understanding of these predilections differs from the prejudices of the present, in which it is the gay man who would wear cosmetics; for the Greeks, so-called 'effeminate' men were like females because they spent so much time with women, and because they longed to seduce them. Manly, military, athletic, outdoorsmen were more likely to pursue boys than women. The two men engage in a rhetorical contest, Charicles defending the heterosexual love of men for women and conceding finally that, if men have intercourse with men, then women should be allowed to same right to love each other, to be 'tribads', that is, 'rubbers', as the Greek has it, women who 'rub' one another:

> Let them strap to themselves cunningly contrived instruments of lechery, those mysterious monstrosities devoid of seed, and let woman lie with woman as does a man. Let wanton Lesbianism [*tribakes aselgeias*, literally 'rubbed licentiousness'] – that word seldom heard, which I feel ashamed even to utter – freely parade itself, and let our women's chambers emulate Philaenis, disgracing themselves with Sapphic amours. And how much better that a woman should invade the provinces of male wantonness than that the nobility of the male sex should become effeminate and play the part of a woman.
>
> (*Affairs of the Heart*, 28; translated by M. D. MacLeod)

Charicles' speech meets with disdain from the defender of male–male love, who insults him by comparing him to women, saying no woman, not 'Telesilla, who armed herself against the Spartiates ... no nor Sappho, the honey-sweet pride of Lesbos', had ever spoken about herself with such zeal as Charicles.

In response to Charicles' praise of women, Callicratidas summons not the goddess Aphrodite, but the boy Eros. Marriage is necessary for reproduction, but as soon as human beings moved beyond the primitive stage of animal breeding, they began to cultivate the aesthetic; man–boy, man–man love, is the aesthetically and philosophically superior form of love. He complains of women's cosmetics, their costumes, their jewels, all concealing an essential repulsiveness. He contrasts the evils associated with women to the manly life of a boy. And, most interestingly, the speech alludes to Sappho's fragment 31, the poem in which she describes sitting across from her beloved and falling apart at the sight. This defence of pederasty by Callicratidas, a man of ancient culture, although written probably almost a thousand years after the time of Sappho, says about loving a boy (46; emphasis added):

> For my part, ye gods of heaven, I pray that it may for ever be my lot in life *to sit opposite my dear one and hear close to me his sweet voice*, to go out when he goes out and share every activity with him.

Lycinus, arbiter of the debate, chooses in favour of Callicratidas, concluding that marriage may be a good thing when it is fortunate, but that philosophers should engage in the love of boys: 'let only the wise be permitted to love boys, for perfect virtue grows least of all among women' (51). Athens, that is, the love of boys, overseen by Eros, triumphs in his view over Corinth and the worship of the goddess Aphrodite. In the framing dialogue Theomnestus complains that it's all very well to love boys 'philosophically', 'to look at the loved one or to listen to his voice as he sits facing you' (53), again alluding to Sappho. But he describes a ladder of pleasure, moving from sight to touch to the kiss, and finally to 'a start with the thighs' and then to striking 'the target'. He cites the consummation of man–boy love of Socrates and Alcibiades, of Achilles who at Patroclus' death mourned 'the intercourse of our thighs', according to the tragedian Aeschylus. Philosophical abstinence, or self-mastery in the presence of a beloved boy, is not recommended. This text, produced in later antiquity, in the fourth century CE, demonstrates the persistence of pederasty, of the philosophical idealisation of man–boy love, a tolerance of same-sex love between women, as well as a misogyny that relegates women to an inferior place in the scale of human beings.

Foucault's work was widely read, and some of those influenced by it and by his activism came to embrace the designation of 'queer', although there were conflicts internal to the movement about whether embracing the pejorative term was a strategically useful move for a liberatory politics. But the terms 'queer theory' and 'queer studies' have gained academic credibility, even as some thinkers have begun to offer critiques of their institutionalisation. Trying to fix and analyse the shifting allegiances, debates and emerging positions in this field may be as difficult as trying to fix the corpus of Sappho as ever-new discoveries of fragments appear to change our understanding of the ancient poet. But it appears that in the field that once was called the history of sexuality, attention has shifted away from historical studies of ancient Greek sexuality to contemporary issues. *The Lesbian and Gay Studies Reader*, published by Routledge in 1993, has copious references to Sappho. David M. Halperin's essay, 'Is there a history of sexuality?', insists on the pertinence of classical antiquity to his question, but following Foucault sees 'sexuality', as a category, as anachronistic when applied to ancient Greece. 'Instead of concentrating our attention specifically on the history of sexuality, then, we need to define and refine a new, and radical, historical sociology of psychology, an intellectual discipline designed to analyse the cultural poetics of desire' (p. 426). The same-sex desire of women, of Sappho, is not at stake per se in his argument. This volume also includes a brilliant and influential essay by the classicist John J. Winkler, who died of AIDS in 1990, entitled 'Double consciousness in Sappho's lyrics'. Winkler insists on the allusive erotic charge of Sappho's poetry; using the concept of cultural bilingualism, the coexistence of two different systems of understanding, he shows that Sappho's verse speaks at the same time to public and private concerns. She sings in light of masculine norms of behaviour, while simultaneously alluding to private realities. Homer constitutes the common cultural tradition; Sappho is conscious, in Winkler's view, of an audience for Homer's work, but also speaks to a private, 'woman-centred' world. Analysing Sappho's fragment 1, the call for Aphrodite to come to the poet's aid, Winkler observes: 'The intensification of both pathos and mastery in the encounter is due largely to the ironic double consciousness of the poet-Sappho speaking in turn the parts of suffering "Sappho" and impassive goddess' (p. 582). Women's consciousness encompasses not only their own private realities, but also the more restricted world of men: 'Sappho's consciousness is a larger circle enclosing the smaller one of Homer' (p. 586). She alludes to 'a sacred landscape of the body', the female body, as in the second poem, in which Aphrodite is summoned to the temple, grove of apples, water shadowed with roses. Sappho's language is both religious and erotic. Winkler's conclusion to this essay is that 'the erotic-lyric tradition' in which Sappho writes, or sings, 'includes pervasive allusions to physical *eros* and that in Sappho's poems both subject and object of shared physical love are women. We now call this lesbian' (p. 592). He definitively rescued Sappho from those who would claim that her desire was not expressed in physical terms, whose 'relentless trivialisation, homophobic anxieties, and sheer misogyny' (p. 577) long infected responses to her work. Yet controversy emerged upon the publication of this volume, as it seemed to some critics to want to distinguish itself from women's studies, feminism and questions of gender.

The *Routledge Queer Studies Reader*, published in 2012, omits Sappho from its index and, although extending its discussion to a wider geographical and ethnically rich set of essays, rarely looks back in time, with the exception of Elizabeth Freeman's 'Turn the beat around: sadomasochism, temporality, history', which locates sadomasochism within 'slow time', a temporality that is pre-capitalist. The former classicist and historian of male homosexuality David M. Halperin also considers historical issues, in his chapter entitled 'How to do the history of male homosexuality', but restricts his discussion to male experience and its description. The recent book *The Lesbian Premodern* (published in 2011, part of The New Middle Ages series) takes up some of these issues. There is a lively debate, in blogs and journal articles as well, concerning 'historicism', about whether the periodising of gay and lesbian and queer studies should reject a genealogical, linear, teleological shape, that is, should these histories and these fields of study add themselves to other forms of history-telling that focus on what came first, what came next, what is now, where are we going?

In general, work on sexuality in the humanities has shifted away from historical concerns to philosophical and social-scientific questions bearing on the present. Melancholy, mourning and loss have come to the forefront of work in studies of culture in the last decade. As more scholars consider exile, diaspora, enslavement, conquest and the sufferings of many in recent history, these categories have enabled some valuable work on culture in the present. The anthology *Loss: The Politics of Mourning* (2002), edited by David Eng and David Kazanjian, takes up these issues, in part spurred by the philosopher Judith Butler, whose recent work has been concerned with questions of mourning: for whom does one mourn, how does one continue to live in a state of ongoing grief? She has written about mourning in relation to HIV/AIDS, to relationships in families that do not correspond to the traditional heterosexual model, to Palestinians vis-à-vis Jewish Israelis, and Jews in the diaspora. *Loss* takes up the categories of Sigmund Freud, in a famous essay called 'Mourning and melancholia', in which he distinguished between a psychically healthy mourning in relation to a loss, on the one hand, in which the subject experiences sadness but, by incorporating memories of the lost one into the psyche, returns eventually to a relatively normal state, and melancholy, on the other hand, which is defined as a pathological state, in which mourning cannot be mastered, in which the loss is perceived as so disabling that one cannot continue to live fully. Eng and Kazanjian seek to modify these categories and these judgements, in part through the work of Walter Benjamin, to come to the understanding that melancholia possesses an open-ended relationship to the past, and that such a continuous engagement with loss may be inevitable, necessary and 'healthy' rather than pathological. Loss, in their view, can be creative: 'Ultimately, such counter-intuitive understandings of loss apprehend the modern and postmodern epoch of loss – characterised by the fragmentation of grand narratives as well as by war, genocide, and neocolonialism' (p. 5). And the losses entailed by a taxonomy of sexual behaviours, and the rejection and persecution of those who practise those officially forbidden, can take on this dimension of creativity as well.

Looking back on the history of the West, these thinkers have seen centuries of trauma. Colonialism brought disaster to the colonised; slavery and racism traumatised vast populations. War has wrought havoc on the survivors as well as those killed. Misogyny, hatred of women, damaged half the world. And homophobia, the fear of homosexuals, the hatred of homosexuality, was among the factors producing loss, mourning and melancholy for many. Although the ancient world of the Greeks and the Romans did not stigmatise homoeroticism, Michel Foucault argued, as noted, that the philosophical turn of the Roman imperial world produced a new cultural synthesis in which any excessive investment in sexual pleasure was viewed negatively, and in which companionate marriage between a man and a woman was seen as a bulwark against a loss of self in eros. In his view, this change came not from Christian moralists bent on asceticism, chastity and celibacy but from the attitudes and mentalities of philosophical and medical thinkers of the Roman Empire.

In any case, the interpretation of the Hebrew Bible by many Christian thinkers led to a disapproval of 'sodomy', erotic behaviour between same-sex partners, even though the Bible contains such intense same-sex attachments as that between David and Jonathan, for example. In 1 Samuel 20:17 the text reads: 'Jonathan made David swear again by his love for him; for he loved him as he loved his own life.' In this same book, Saul attacks Jonathan: 'You son of a perverse, rebellious woman! Do I not know that you have chosen the son of Jesse [David] to your own shame, and to the shame of your mother's nakedness?' (1 Samuel 20:30). Such passages were interpreted not as signs of sexual connection between the two heroes but as expressing political loyalty, in the Christian era, and other contradictory passages in the Bible were chosen to define morality. The priestly book Leviticus, for example, focused on ritual purity, forbidding incest, intercourse with a menstruating woman, adultery with a kinsman's wife, and adding: 'You shall not lie with a male as with a woman; it is an abomination.' Those who occupied the land before the Israelites did are said to have committed all these abominations, and the land itself became defiled. In what is known as the 'New Testament', the second part of the Christian Bible, Jesus says nothing about homosexuality, and some have argued that 'the man whom Jesus loved' is in fact his beloved. But the Jewish apostle Paul, follower of Jesus, in his letter to the Romans denounced the sexual practices of Rome;

those who did not come to monotheism and worship of the one god through observation of his power and divine nature became fools, and the god gave them up to impurity:

> Their women exchanged natural intercourse for unnatural, and in the same way also the men, giving up natural intercourse with women, were consumed with passion for one another. Men committed shameless acts with men and received in their own persons the due penalty for their error.
>
> (Romans 1:26–7)

These views came to dominate the institution of the Christian Church, even though some scholars have presented evidence concerning special friendships between men and men, women with women, and even ceremonies resembling weddings between same-sex partners.

Throughout the Christian era, however, same-sex eros has been officially disapproved of and persecuted, seen as 'sodomy', for example, a sin to be confessed (even though the episode of Sodom in the Old Testament book of Genesis has been interpreted as a failure of hospitality by the Sodomites rather than a sexual crime, and even though Lot offers his own daughters, with whom he later commits incest, to the men of Sodom who want to 'know' Lot's angelic guests (Genesis 19)). Michel Foucault's argument is that before nineteenth-century sexologists and psychoanalysts began the process of diagnosing and medicalising what they saw as sexual deviance, as pathologies, same-sex eros, although not officially approved of, did not define the *identity* of a person who acted on same-sex desire.

Recent academic work has moved from the discovery of lesbian and gay presence in the historical periods since the fall of Roman antiquity to an exploration of the multiplicity of forms of 'queerness'. In relation to new work on 'affect', on subjective experience, emotions, 'feelings', some queer scholars, or scholars of queerness, have written about loss, about the melancholy of exclusion from so-called 'heteronormativity', that is, the requirement implicit or explicit in societies that require everyone to find a mate of the opposite sex, marry and produce offspring. Judith Butler's

Antigone's Claim: Kinship between Life and Death (2000), for example, is a beautiful and extended meditation on this question. She considers the place of Oedipus in Freud's psychoanalytic theory, and questions what changes would result from a focus not on Oedipus, but rather on his incestuously produced daughter Antigone, his sister as well as his daughter, born from his union with his own mother. Antigone is eloquent in a world where women rarely address the powerful, she remains profoundly attached to her brother rather than to her betrothed and she is silenced by Creon, ruler of Thebes, who orders that she be shut alive into a tomb for her attempt ritually to bury her dead brother. She commits suicide, as does her betrothed, and the world of Creon is destroyed. Butler considers Antigone's place, outside the 'norm', and writes movingly of the melancholy that comes to those in contemporary culture who live in other sorts of families, same-sex couples with children, partners whose losses include the death of loved ones with HIV/AIDS, all those whose right to mourn, to have acknowledged their familial, affective ties, are denied by law.

Two recent books, *Feeling Backward: Loss and the Politics of Queer History* (2007) by Heather Love and *Getting Medieval* (1999) by Carolyn Dinshaw, might serve as examples of new work in this field that obliquely cast light on our understanding of Sappho and her poetry in the twenty-first century CE. In *Feeling Backward* Heather Love develops further themes of loss and exclusion. 'For groups constituted by historical injury, the challenge is to engage with the past without being destroyed by it ... The history of Western representation is littered with the corpses of gender and sexual deviants. Those who are directly identified with same-sex desire most often end up dead' (p. 1). Love is angry, and determined to remind those who ignore these facts, who seek to attribute them only to propagandists against homoeroticism, that the depressing accounts of life lived under conditions of persecution and injury must be reckoned with. Love's text is 'populated by iconic figures that turn backward' (p. 5). She lists Lot's wife, who turns back towards Sodom and Gomorrah and is turned into a pillar of salt; Orpheus who looks backwards to his Eurydice as he leaves the underworld, and loses her; Ulysses who gazes backwards at the singing Sirens as his crew of rowers pulls away from the threat they embody; and others. She constructs 'an archive of feeling', attending to 'nostalgia, regret, shame, despair, *ressentiment*, passivity, escapism, self-hatred, withdrawal, bitterness, defeatism, and loneliness' (p. 4). Her chapters focus on texts by Walter Pater, Willa Cather, Radclyffe Hall and Sylvia Townsend Warner, who express such feelings, and bear witness to the toll taken on these gifted and sensitive writers by a pervasive and invasive homophobia. Her work on Walter Pater, nineteenth-century critic, novelist and English academic, explores his sadness, his sense of exclusion from the modern world and his withdrawal into aestheticism and nostalgia for a lost past. Love calls his 'a backward modernism', resistant to the revolutionary impulses of his day, as Pater retreated into secrecy and a sense of the value of victimisation. There is a heroism of martyrdom in his world, in *Marius the Epicurean: His Sensations and Ideas* (1885), a novel that presents the life of a young man living in the second century CE, during the Roman Empire. Growing up in the countryside of Italy, Marius is educated in a boarding school, and as a young man is attracted to the philosophical school of Epicurus, which is not the advocacy of pure pleasure we might now associate with the term 'epicurean'. Pleasure, in the sense in which it used here, is the absence of pain. In antiquity, Epicurus and his followers, including Aristippus, stood for a serenity that faced adversity or pleasure with equanimity, and that preferred retreat to a garden of contemplation and peace over engagement with public life, with the struggles of a political world. The goal was mastery of the self, rather than enslavement to the passions; committed not to an austere refusal of pleasures, the epicurean was appreciative of beauty, human and otherwise, but not its slave. Tranquillity of the soul, an unruffled state, were seen as the greatest good, and friendship among those who followed these teachings occupied an important place.

In Pater's novel Marius becomes the secretary of the emperor Marcus Aurelius, an adherent of the rival philosophical school, Stoicism, which stressed reason over emotion, acceptance of one's position in the universe and therefore engagement if necessary with public and political existence. Marius becomes disillusioned with the spectacles of Rome and even with the philosophical attitude of the emperor himself, a Stoicism which ultimately proves to be arid and lacking in compassion, for example, for the animals and human beings who suffer in the arena. He finds himself on the fringes of a new cult, the followers of Jesus, and although he never converts to their beliefs, he allows himself to be captured by those who think he is part of this group and he dies with the consolations of his own code, one of epicurean asceticism and selfless love.

Love, in *Feeling Backward*, interprets Pater's 'backward modernism' as a gaze into the past, like that of Lot's wife, or Eurydice. She calls for a politics in the present that is not revolutionary confrontation, but a rethinking of the relationship between power and the powerless. '[Q]ueer subjects might begin to forge a politics that keeps faith with those who drew back and those whose names were forgotten ... we need to recognize and even affirm forms of ruined political subjectivity ... we need a politics forged in the image of exile, of refusal, even of failure' (p. 71). But we might also see Pater's fascination with Marius as a liberating investment in a world that had not yet come to stigmatise erotic experience between men. Although Marius falls into the orbit of the early Christians, and has intimations of what will become the dominant religious system of Europe in the centuries to come, he does not convert to Christianity. And his attachment to his boyhood friend Flavianus, who dies after attending a festival of Isis, precedes another significant emotional bond with the man Cornelius. Marius travels with Cornelius, they are captured together and Marius allows himself to be taken for a Christian, which allows Cornelius to escape captivity as Marius martyrs himself for friendship or love, not for adherence to the new religion. It is love, love of these male companions, that enriches his life and that provides him with solace at the end. Even though Pater writes that Marius' soul was 'naturally Christian', the character remains a pagan, an epicurean. Rather than seeing an interest in pre-Christian 'paganism' as a form of dispirited melancholy, a despairing attachment to earlier, now transcended and impossibly distant social arrangements concerning sexuality, one might reconsider the possibilities inherent in looking backwards differently. That is, looking backward not just to the suffering and depression of gay and lesbian and queer persecution, but also to the model of an ancient world in which the structures of heterosexual norms, punishment, confession and secrecy had not yet been instituted in the name of the one god.

The work of the medievalist Carolyn Dinshaw can also cast light on new ways of conceptualising historical 'periods', and the relationship between past and present. In *Getting Medieval*, the title of which refers to Quentin Tarantino's film *Pulp Fiction*, Dinshaw elaborates on the themes of her subtitle: *Sexualities and Communities, Pre- and Postmodern*. Presenting a model of 'partial connections between incommensurate entities' (p. 54), she rejects not only a notion of imitation in relation to other times, other places, other 'identities', but also a sense of an impassable chasm between pasts and presents. Her focus in this book is on 'sex', but she follows what she calls 'a queer historical impulse, an impulse toward making connections across time between, on the one hand, lives, texts, and other cultural phenomena left out of sexual categories back then and, on the other, those left out of current sexual categories now'. Her arguments are in part a response to earlier debates in gay and lesbian studies that pitted 'essentialists' against 'constructivists', that is, those who believed that there always were, always have been gay and lesbian people, and those who saw such identities as historically constructed, as in the identification of some persons as 'homosexual' in the nineteenth century. She seeks to 'explode the categories of sameness, otherness, present, past, loss, pleasure' (p. 2), and she proposes a 'contingent history', playing on the double meaning of the word 'contingent', which can mean both 'subject to chance' and 'touching'. In late-medieval England she finds partial connections with the present, inventing 'new times', a new way of doing history and new ways of acting in queer politics.

One cannot look at the history of the post-classical era and not feel anguish at the sufferings of its victims, the colonised, the racialised and those stigmatised by the norms of heterosexuality. But in a sense it may be that we are not looking backward enough, not far enough. In the implicit structuring of modern and postmodern societies by monotheism, and by the moralisms of Abrahamic religions, that is, Judaism, Christianity and Islam, Western societies continue to be haunted by the Hebrew Bible and by misreadings of its strictures. In my book *A Million and One Gods: The Persistence of Polytheism* (2014), I take on the ways in which even atheists, agnostics and those indifferent to religion, in the West, in the US and UK, live within a monotheist paradigm. The so-called separation of church and state that came as a result of the persecution of Protestant dissenters in the sixteenth and seventeenth centuries produced not tolerance, but an implicit adherence to political structures that serve to protect monotheism. Inscribed on the money of the US is the slogan 'In God We Trust.' The sovereign of the United Kingdom and the Commonwealth is the head of *The* Church of England, sovereign over her or his subjects. Prayers conducted by religious leaders to open deliberations in Congress and Parliament are usually led by those affirming monotheism and the tradition of belief that descends from Abraham, that is, Christians, Jews and Muslims. Although these religious communities may often be at odds with one another, violently or not, they belong to just one of the families of religions in the world. Moreover, their 'monotheism' is somewhat illusory; some Christian communities worship the entities that make up a trinity – Father, Son and Holy Spirit – and fear the deity of evil, Satan. Jews revere the patriarchs. Muslims acknowledge the powers of supernatural beings, deities, djinns, angels and the devil. But in any case, there are communities not bound to a pseudo-monotheism, such as the growing population of Hindus in both the UK and the US. And it may be that the structures of political life, the forms of guilt, shame, confession, repentance and redemption that accompany monotheism, contribute to the persecution of gay and lesbian, transsexual, transvestite and other queer residents in these ostensibly monotheistic countries where the legacy of the Hebrew Bible, its condemnations and its misreading, continues to justify these forms of persecution, even as these societies consider themselves to be ever more secular.

We cannot of course turn back to the utopianism and ecstatic writing of the lesbian and feminist writers of the 1970s without some qualms. Their ecstasies and hopes for absolute and definitive revolution may seem overheated, even slightly ridiculous now. Nonetheless, the attempt to escape from the sadness and depression and moralism of religious and legal controls over the expression of sexuality had their impact on the social movements of their day. I would argue that looking further back, to 'paganism', to polytheism and to ancient Greek and Roman sexual life, seeing clearly how much the world of the present is limited in its imagination by being still embedded in the culture of shame, sin and confession that comes with monotheism, might be a path forward. Sappho should be a part of the mental universe of the present just as much as Radclyffe Hall and looking to the recent past, or to a Christian, post-Renaissance, homophobic environment, where sexual life is managed in light of a misreading of rules that come from 3,000 years ago, needs to be undermined. Although study of the humanities increasingly turns away from history, and perhaps especially from ancient history, this is an unforgivable loss, a loss of human possibility, of critique of the present, of an opening to a wider universe of feeling. Some might consider such a call naïve, insufficiently aware of present and recent suffering, utopian and cavalier about the weight of institutions and culture and history that would prohibit such an opening. But these thinkers themselves might refuse a passive acceptance of the inevitability of melancholy, or use melancholy, its persistence, to refuse the moralism of an implicit monotheism, a judge and a judgement that inhibit creative and utopian imaginings.

When we look back to Sappho's fragment 1, the poem in the first chapter of this book, a hymn to Aphrodite beseeching her aid again in turning an object of desire into a subject, how does all that intervenes in the 2,500 years since it was composed help us to understand better the poet and her poem? If we are moved by queer theory's appeal to 'contingent histories', new modes of connecting with archaic Lesbos and its legacy might extend beyond polytheism, ancient sexualities, Lesbian/lesbian/sapphic erotics and poetics, to myriad enriching forms of contact between the archaic past, our present, the future.

Sources and Suggestions for Further Reading

This is a partial, selective list of works that I consulted in writing this book, and that might be of interest to those desiring to read more about Sappho.

INTRODUCTION AND CHAPTER 1

The most accessible version of Sappho and her contemporary Alkaios comes from the Loeb Classical Library, with facing Greek text and English translation. Volume 142 in this series is *Greek Lyric I: Sappho and Alcaeus* (using the Latin spelling of the poet's name, as is common), edited and translated by David A. Campbell. Also recommended is *Reading Sappho: Contemporary Approaches*, edited by Ellen Greene. The translations of John Daley can be found in his *Poetry of Sappho*, introduction by Page duBois, except for the translations of the most recently discovered fragments, which are published only here.

Bray, Alan, *Homosexuality in Renaissance England* (London: Gay Men's Press, 1982).
Budelmann, Felix (ed.), *The Cambridge Companion to Greek Lyric* (Cambridge: Cambridge University Press, 2009).

Sources and Suggestions for Further Reading

Calame, Claude, *Choruses of Young Women in Ancient Greece*, trans. Derek Collins and Janice Orion (Lanham, MD: Rowman & Littlefield, 1997).

Campbell, David A. (ed. and trans.), *Greek Lyric: I, Sappho and Alcaeus*, Loeb Classical Library 142 (Cambridge, MA: Harvard University Press, 1982, reprinted 1990).

Carson, Anne, *Eros the Bittersweet* (Baltimore, MD: Johns Hopkins University Press, 1986).

——*If Not, Winter: Fragments of Sappho* (New York, NY: Knopf, 2002).

Daley, John, *Poetry of Sappho*, introduction by Page duBois; in Greek with English translation by John Daley with Page duBois; prints by Julie Mehretu, wood engravings by Anita Cowles Rearden (San Francisco, CA: Arion Press, 2011).

duBois, Page, *Sappho Is Burning* (Chicago, IL: University of Chicago Press, 1997).

Ferrari, Franco, *Sappho's Gift: The Poet and Her Community*, trans. Benjamin Acosta-Hughes and Lucia Prauscello (Ann Arbor, MI: Michigan Classical Press, 2010).

Foucault, Michel, *History of Sexuality*, vol. 1, *An Introduction*, trans. Robert Hurley (New York, NY: Vintage, 1980).

——*History of Sexuality*, vol. 2, *The Use of Pleasure*, trans. Robert Hurley (New York, NY: Vintage, 1990).

——*History of Sexuality*, vol. 3, *The Care of the Self*, trans. Robert Hurley (New York, NY: Vintage, 1988).

Graziano, Frank (ed.), *Alejandra Pizarnik: A Profile* (Durango, CO: Logbridge-Rhodes, 1987).

Greene, Ellen (ed.), *Reading Sappho: Contemporary Approaches* (Berkeley, CA: University of California Press, 1996).

Halperin, David M., John J. Winkler and Froma I. Zeitlin (eds), *Before Sexuality: The Construction of Erotic Experience in the Ancient Greek World* (Princeton, NJ: Princeton University Press, 1990).

Johnson, Marguerite, *Ancients in Action: Sappho* (Bristol: Bristol Classical Press, 2007).

McClure, Laura (ed.), *Sexuality and Gender in the Classical World: Readings and Sources* (Oxford: Blackwell, 2002).

Page, Denys, *Sappho and Alcaeus* (Oxford: Oxford University Press, 1955).

Roche, Paul (trans.), *The Love Songs of Sappho, with an introduction by Page duBois* (Amherst, NY: Prometheus Books, 1998; 1st edn 1984).

Segal, Charles, *Aglaia: The Poetry of Alcman, Sappho, Pindar, Bacchylides, and Corinna* (Lanham, MD: Rowman & Littlefield, 1998).

Skinner, Marilyn B., *Sexuality in Greek and Roman Culture* (Oxford: Blackwell, 2005).

Snyder, Jane M., *Lesbian Desire in the Lyrics of Sappho* (New York, NY: Columbia University Press, 1998).

Voigt, Eva-Maria, *Sappho et Alcaeus* (Amsterdam: Athenaeum-Polak and van Gennep, 1971).

Sources and Suggestions for Further Reading

Williamson, Margaret, *Sappho's Immortal Daughters* (Cambridge, MA: Harvard University Press, 1995).

Wittig, Monique, *Les Guérillères*, trans. David Le Vay (Boston, MA: Beacon Press, 1985).

CHAPTERS 2, 3 AND 4

Ancient sources concerning the life of Sappho are listed in David A. Campbell's *Sappho and Alcaeus*. Also very useful is Claude Calame, *Choruses of Young Women in Ancient Greece*. Anne Carson's *If Not, Winter: Fragments of Sappho* contains all the fragments known to that point. The works of the other ancient Greek lyric poets have been edited and translated in David Campbell's *Greek Lyric II–V*. The translations that I prefer of the works of Homer are those of Richmond Lattimore.

On the early reception of Sappho, see Dimitrios Yatromanolakis, *Sappho in the Making*. The Loeb Classical Library is always useful for translations of Roman poets, especially Catullus' poems, Ovid's *Heroides* and *Amores*. Also very worthwhile is the volume edited by Ellen Greene entitled *Re-Reading Sappho: Reception and Transmission*.

There are many generations of translators of Sappho. See the more recent volumes published by John Daley, Anne Carson and Mary Barnard. For more information on the traditions of reception and translation, consult Ellen Greene's invaluable *Re-Reading Sappho*. For an excellent set of essays on one of the most recently discovered fragments, see *The New Sappho on Old Age: Textual and Philosophical Issues*, edited by Ellen Greene and Marilyn B. Skinner. For their histories, see Margaret Reynolds' *The Sappho Companion* and *The Sappho History*.

Plutarch's *Dialogue on Love* comes from Plutarch, *Moralia*, vol. 9, translated by E. L. Minar, Jr., F. H. Sandbach and W. C. Helmbold (Cambridge, MA: Harvard University Press, 1961). Citations from Plato come from *The Collected Dialogues of Plato, including the Letters*, ed. Edith Hamilton and Huntington Cairns (Princeton, NJ: Princeton University Press, 1961).

Unless otherwise noted, translations are the author's own.

Sources and Suggestions for Further Reading

Athanassakis, Apostolos N. (trans.), *The Homeric Hymns*, 2nd edn (Baltimore, MD: Johns Hopkins University Press, 2004).
Barnard, Mary, *Sappho: A New Translation* (Berkeley, CA: University of California Press, 1958).
Boehringer, Sandra, *L'Homosexualité féminine dans l'antiquité grecque et romaine* (Paris: Les Belles Lettres, 2007).
Bryher, *The Heart to Artemis: A Writer's Memoirs* (Ashfield, MA: Paris Press, 2006).
Calame, Claude, *Choruses of Young Women in Ancient Greece*, trans. Derek Collins and Janice Orion (Lanham, MD: Rowman & Littlefield, 1997).
Campbell, David A. (ed. and trans.), *Greek Lyric: I, Sappho and Alcaeus*, Loeb Classical Library 142 (Cambridge, MA: Harvard University Press, 1982).
—— *Greek Lyric: II, Anacreon, Anacreontea, Early Choral Lyric*, Loeb Classical Library 143 (Cambridge, MA: Harvard University Press, 1988).
—— *Greek Lyric: III, Stesichorus, Ibycus, Simonides*, Loeb Classical Library 476 (Cambridge, MA: Harvard University Press, 1991).
—— *Greek Lyric: IV, Bacchylides, Corinna, and Others*, Loeb Classical Library 461 (Cambridge, MA: Harvard University Press, 1992).
—— *Greek Lyric: V, The New School of Poetry and Anonymous Songs and Hymns*, Loeb Classical Library 144 (Cambridge, MA: Harvard University Press, 1993).
Carson, Anne, *If Not, Winter: Fragments of Sappho* (New York, NY: Knopf, 2002).
Catullus, Tibullus, *Pervigilium Veneris*, trans. F. W. Cornish, J. P. Postgate and J. W. Mackail, revised by G. P. Goold, Loeb Classical Library 6 (Cambridge, MA: Harvard University Press, 1995).
DeJean, Joan, *Fictions of Sappho, 1546–1937* (Chicago: University of Chicago Press, 1989).
Fagles, Robert, *Homer: The Iliad* (New York, NY: Penguin, 1990).
Goldhill, Simon, *Victorian Culture and Classical Antiquity: Art, Opera, Fiction, and the Proclamation of Modernity* (Princeton, NJ: Princeton University Press, 2011).
Grahn, Judy, *The Highest Apple: Sappho and The Lesbian Poetic Tradition* (San Francisco, CA: Spinsters, Ink, 1985).
Greene, Ellen (ed.), *Re-Reading Sappho: Reception and Transmission* (Berkeley, CA: University of California Press, 1996).
Greene, Ellen, and Marilyn B. Skinner (eds), *The New Sappho on Old Age: Textual and Philosophical Issues* (Washington, DC: Center for Hellenic Studies, Trustees for Harvard University, 2009).
Irigaray, Luce, *This Sex Which Is Not One*, trans. Catherine Porter with Carolyn Burke (Ithaca, NY: Cornell University Press, 1985).
Lattimore, Richmond, *The Iliad of Homer* (Chicago, IL: University of Chicago Press, 1961; reprinted 2011).
—— *The Odyssey of Homer* (New York, NY: Harper & Row, 1965; reprinted 2007).

Peri Rossi, Cristina, *Evohé: poemas eróticos/Erotic Poems*, trans. Diana P. Decker (Washington, DC: Azul Editions, 1994).
Prins, Yopie, *Victorian Sappho* (Princeton, NJ: Princeton University Press, 1999).
Rayor, Diane (trans.), *Sappho's Lyre: Archaic Lyric and Women Poets of Ancient Greece* (Berkeley, CA: University of California Press, 1991).
Reynolds, Margaret, *The Sappho Companion* (London: Palgrave Macmillan, 2001).
—— *The Sappho History* (London: Palgrave Macmillan, 2003).
Showerman, Grant, *Ovid, I: Heroides, Amores* (rev. G. P. Goold), Loeb Classical Library 41 (Cambridge, MA: Harvard University Press, 1914).
Turner, Frank, *The Greek Heritage in Victorian Britain* (New Haven, CT: Yale University Press, 1981).
Vanita, Ruth, *Sappho and the Virgin Mary: Same-Sex Love and the English Literary Imagination* (New York, NY: Columbia University Press, 1996).
Yatromanolakis, Dimitrios, *Sappho in the Making: The Early Reception* (Washington, DC: Center for Hellenic Studies, Trustees for Harvard University Press, 2007).

CHAPTER 5

There are many resources on the development and current state of queer theory. Among the best are *The Lesbian and Gay Studies Reader*, edited by Henry Abelove, Michèle Aina Barale and David M. Halperin, and *The Routledge Queer Studies Reader*, edited by Donald E. Hall and Annamarie Jagose, with Andrea Bebell and Susan Potter. Other sources, including the works of Monique Wittig and H. D., are noted in the text of Chapter 5 and below.

Abelove, Henry, Michèle Aina Barale and David M. Halperin (eds), *The Lesbian and Gay Studies Reader* (New York, NY, and London: Routledge, 1993).
Dinshaw, Carolyn, *Getting Medieval: Sexualities and Communities, Pre- and Postmodern* (Durham, NC: Duke University Press, 1999).
—— *How Soon Is Now? Medieval Texts, Amateur Readers, and the Queerness of Time* (Durham, NC: Duke University Press, 2012).
Eng, David L., and David Kazanjian (eds), *Loss: The Politics of Mourning* (Berkeley, CA: University of California Press, 2003).
Goldberg, Jonathan (ed.), *Queering the Renaissance* (Durham, NC: Duke University Press, 1994).
Hall, Donald E., and Annamarie Jagose, with Andrea Bebell and Susan Potter (eds), *The Routledge Queer Studies Reader* (London: Routledge, 2013).

Halperin, David M., 'Is there a history of sexuality?', in H. Abelove et al. (eds), pp. 416–31.

H. D., *Notes on Thought & Vision & The Wise Sappho* (San Francisco, CA: City Lights Books, 1982).

Love, Heather, *Feeling Backward: Loss and the Politics of Queer History* (Cambridge, MA: Harvard University Press, 2007).

MacLeod, M. D., *Lucian: VIII*, Loeb Classical Library 432 (Cambridge, MA: Harvard University Press, 1967).

Nissinen, Martti, *Homoeroticism in the Biblical World: A Historical Perspective*, trans. Kirsi Stjerna (Minneapolis, MN: Fortress Press, 1998).

Winkler, John J., 'Double consciousness in Sappho's lyrics', in H. Abelove et al. (eds), pp. 577–94.

Wittig, Monique, *The Lesbian Body*, trans. David LeVay (New York: William Morrow, 1975).

Index

Abrahamic religions, 171–2
Addington Symonds, John, 122, 142
Addison, John, 141
Adonis, 66, 67, 88–9, 148
Aeneas (Aineias), 11, 21, 106
affect, 167, 168–70, 173
Africa, 84, 102, 146
  see also Egypt
ageing, 113, 146–9
Akhilleus (Achilles), 20, 26, 28, 37, 39, 41, 42–3, 58, 162
Alexandria, 67, 97–9, 110
Alkaios (Alcaeus), 33, 35, 43, 47, 72, 76, 78–9, 86, 94, 114, 133, 137
Allen, Paula Gunn, 130–1
Alma-Tadema, Laurence, 127
alpha-privative, 22, 26
Amaterasu, 155
Amazons, 37, 80, 140, 156
Anakreon (Anacreon), 23, 85, 88, 140
Anaktoria, 48, 96, 108, 126, 138, 156
Andreadis, Harriet, 119
Andromakhe (Andromache), 38
Antigone, 168
Anyte, 87, 140
Aphrodite, 11, 12, 13, 21, 23, 25, 57, 88, 95, 108, 138, 148, 162
  birth of, 10–11
  in Sappho's fragments, 7, 10, 15, 17–18, 47, 58–9, 60, 64–5, 74, 151, 173
  worship of, 11, 14, 16, 31, 64, 66, 74, 137, 151
Apollo, 53, 72, 88, 109, 133, 139
Apollonios Rhodios, 100
Arcadia, 87
Argonautika, The, 100–1
aristocracy, 77–8, 90, 102, 122
Aristotle, 79, 97, 133
Aristophanes, 51, 54, 73, 91, 159
Arkhilokhos (Archilochus), 62, 72, 106
Artemis, 16, 27, 55, 66, 128
Ashbery, John, 145
Asherah, 130
Asia, 9, 11, 35–6, 38, 52, 57, 59, 66, 76, 83, 97–8, 129
Asianism, 9
Astarte, 11, 14, 66, 108, 157
Athena, 18, 21
Athens, 78, 90–2
Athenaios (Athenaeus), 62, 66, 69, 79, 86
Atthis, 55, 71, 108, 137–8, 142

Bacchus, 131–2
  see also Dionysos
Bantock, Granville, 134–5

181

Index

Barnard, Mary, 55, 143
Barney, Natalie, 123–4
Baudelaire, Charles, 123
Behn, Aphra, 120
bel canto, 133–4
Bellini, Vincenzo, 133–4
black earth, 18, 20, 45, 157
Boileau, Nicolas, 114, 140
Botticelli, Sandro, *Birth of Venus*, 14
Bray, Alan, 120
brothers, Sappho's, 82, 108–9, 138, 139, 150–3
'brothers fragment', 151–2
Bryher, 128
Bunting, Basil, 143
Butler, Judith, 165, 167–8
Byron, George Gordon, 141–2

Campbell, David, 143
Campion, Thomas, 142
Carson, Anne, 144, 153
castrati, 133
Catullus, 102–5, 121, 129, 140
Chicago, Judy, 158
Christianity, 107, 110–11, 113, 123, 166–7, 170
cicadas, 148–9
Cicero, 80
Cihuacoatl, 155
Cixous, Hélène, 124, 155
comedy, 81, 90–3
  Sappho in, 91–3
Crete, 51, 64
Cyprus, Cyprian, 11, 14, 65–6, 82, 150

Daley, John, 113, 140, 144–6, 150–3
dance, 54, 138, 146, 155
David, Jacques-Louis, 127
David and Jonathan, 110
death, 40–2, 48, 59, 67, 88, 99, 106
DeJean, Joan, 120–4
Demeter, 34
democracy, 78, 90
Dickinson, Emily, 130
Dido, 104, 106, 108
dildo, 72–3, 161
Dinshaw, Carolyn, 168, 171

Diomedes, 18
Dionysios of Halikarnassos, 9, 113
Dionysos, 75–6, 90–1
Donizetti, Gaetano, 133–4
Donne, John, 115–19, 139
Doolittle, Hilda (H. D.), 127–30
Dorikha, 83–4, 138, 150–2
Dorn, Edward, 145

effeminacy, 161
Egypt, 38, 43–4, 53, 62, 80, 83–4, 97–8, 101, 109, 111, 113–14, 129, 142, 152
Eliot, T. S., 148
Eos (Dawn, Day), 21, 70, 147–8
epic, 36
  see also Homer
epicureanism, 169
epigrams, 86–7, 98
epithalamia, 68–71
Erinna, 86
eros, 22, 29, 42, 47, 51, 79, 82, 95–6, 101, 132, 144, 150, 155, 156, 159, 164, 166, 167
Eros the god, 12, 23, 74, 77, 85, 95, 147, 159–60, 162
exile, 80, 131, 132, 133, 165

family, 35, 39, 44–6, 68, 82–3, 108, 113, 121, 138, 150–3, 165
feminism, 127
Field, Michael, 125
flogging, 125–6
flowers, 55, 57–8, 59–62, 64–5, 68, 70–1, 104, 116, 130, 149
Foucault, Michel, 107, 158, 160, 163, 166, 167
France, 114, 120–4
frankincense, 39, 64
Freud, Sigmund, 128, 165, 168

Gaia, 10, 20
Germany, 122–3
Goldhill, Simon, 126–7
Gounod, Charles, 132–3, 134
Grahn, Judy, 130–1
Greek Anthology, 117

Index

Green, Peter, 136–9
  Laughter of Aphrodite, The, 136–9
green fear, 42
Greene, Ellen, 119
Gregory, Eileen, 128
Grenfell, Bernard and Arthur Hunt, 114
Grillparzer, Franz, 122

Hall, Radclyffe, 169, 173
Halperin, David M., 163–4
Hebrew Bible, 98, 110, 166–7, 171–2
Helen, 13, 29, 34, 42–4, 46–9, 95
Hellanikos of Lesbos, 148
Hellenistic poetry, 83, 98–102
henotheism, 74
Hephaistion, 9, 67
Hephaistos, 13, 58
Hera, 25, 57, 75–7, 87, 89, 151–2
Herakles, 34, 43
Hermes, 69, 88
Herodas, 73
Herodotos, 53, 81, 83, 98, 150
Hesiod, 10–11, 30
hieros gamos, 25
himeros, 30, 96
Hindus, 74, 172
historicism, 164, 171
HIV/AIDS, 158, 163, 168
Homer, 12, 18, 36, 163
  Iliad, 18, 19, 20, 21, 25, 26, 28, 29, 31, 36–7, 41, 42, 56, 57
  Odyssey, 19, 30, 36–7, 41, 43, 47, 55, 76, 88
Homeric Hymn to Aphrodite, 11, 21, 147–8
homoeroticism, 6, 40–1, 50–1, 107, 115, 119–28, 136, 160, 166, 168
homophobia, 166
Horace, 106–7, 160

Inanna, 11, 14, 66, 67
Irigaray, Luce, 115, 124–5, 155
Ishtar, 11, 14, 66, 67, 157
Isis, 114

Jesus, 110, 166–7, 170
Juvenal, 159

Kharaxos, 82–4, 138, 150–3
Kleis (Cleis), 35, 54, 121, 129, 138
Korinna (Corinna), 85
Kristeva, Julia, 124–5

law, 26
Lesbia, 104, 125
Lesbian/lesbian, 157, 164
Lesbos, 6, 11, 23, 35, 76, 86, 123, 129, 137, 156
Leukas (Leucas), 88, 109, 141–2
Longinus, 39, 140
Lorde, Audre, 130
Louys, Pierre, 123
Love, Heather, 168–70
Lowell, Amy, 130
Lucian, 117, 160
  Affairs of the Heart, 160–2
luxury, 38–9, 53–4, 58–60, 62, 64–5, 147, 150
Lydia, Lydians, 45, 49, 52–4, 84
Lyly, John, 119
lyric, 36, 42

marriage, 38–9, 44, 76–7, 79–80, 159–60, 162
Martial, 117
masturbation, 109, 117, 118
Medea, 100–1, 108
Mediterranean Sea, 37, 44, 52–3, 55, 56–7, 64, 75–6, 82–4, 152
Meleager, 128
Menander, 88–9, 91–2, 114
Menelaos, 37, 41, 42, 75, 78
Meroe, 146
Million and One Gods, A, 171
misogyny, 166
monotheism, 74, 167, 171–3
moon, 56–7
mourning and melancholia, 165, 167–8, 173
Muses, 72, 74, 77, 85, 95, 97, 98, 101, 104, 106, 110, 138, 146, 149, 159
myrrh, 39, 64

Index

Myrtis, 85
Mytilene, 35–6, 77–9, 84, 87, 137

Nagy, Gregory, 89–90
Newcastle, Duchess of, 120
Nossis, 86
Notley, Alice, 145

Odysseus, 13, 15, 37, 55
  see also Homer: *Odyssey*
Olympiads, 34
opera, 132–6
Ouranos, 10, 20
Ovid, 107–10, 119–21, 126, 139
Oxyrhynchus, 114

Pacini, Giovanni, 132–3
Page, Denys, 63
Palatine Anthology, 77, 86–7, 98–9
Pan, 87
papyri, 68, 111, 114, 142
Parian Marble, 80
pastoral, 56, 64–5, 70–1, 87, 140
Pater, Walter, 169–70
Paul, 110, 166–7
pederasty, 28, 29, 51, 125, 131, 162
Peloponnesos, 34
Penelope, 13, 14, 19, 56, 88, 108
Peri Rossi, Cristina, 131–2
Phaethon, 89
Phaon, 88, 108–10, 115, 133–5, 137, 148
Philaenis, 115–19, 161
Philips, Katherine, 119
philology, 123
Pittakos, 35, 78–9, 138
Pizarnik, Alejandra, 131
Plato, 11, 23, 43, 45–6, 50–1, 81, 94–7, 129, 160
  Phaedrus, 43, 95–7, 148–9
Plutarch, 86, 159–60
polytheism, 63, 73–4, 97, 172–3
Pope, Alexander, 120
Poseidon, 34
pothos, 63, 96
Pound, Ezra, 55, 127, 142–3, 144
Poussin, Nicolas, 87

Praxilla, 86
Prins, Yopie, 125–6, 139
Psappho, 26, 29, 156
psychoanalysis, 40, 128, 158, 165, 168
pursuit and flight, 19, 26–7, 31, 41, 90, 94

queer/queer theory, 155, 158, 163–5

Racine, Jean, 121, 140
Rayor, Diane, 143–4
reception, 127, 153
Renaissance, 114
rhetoric, 9, 97, 161
Rhodopis, 83–4, 129, 150–2
Rich, Adrienne, 130
Robeson, Paul, 128
Roche, Paul, 144
Rome, 101–11, 113, 129, 159, 166–7, 169–70
Ronsard, Pierre de, 140

Salinger, J. D., 69
Salonen, Esa-Pekka, 135–6
Sanskrit, 57, 89
'Sapho 1900', 124, 155
Sappho, fragments of,
  fragment 1, 7–32, 36, 41, 48, 60–1, 73, 79, 94, 104, 131, 145, 163–4, 173
  fragment 2, 64–6, 126, 164
  fragment 5, 82, 150–3
  fragment 7, 83, 150
  fragment 15, 83
  fragment 16, 44–9, 52, 96, 101, 144
  fragment 17, 75–7
  fragment 22, 101
  fragment 26, 150
  fragment 27, 68
  fragment 30, 68–9
  fragment 31, 39–42, 95–6, 100–1, 104–5, 108–9, 113–14, 120–1, 125, 139–44, 159, 162
  fragment 39, 54
  fragment 44, 38
  fragment 47, 74
  fragment 51, 140
  fragment 55, 71–2

Index

fragment 57, 71
fragment 58, 146–7, 149
fragment 94, 59–64, 138
fragment 96, 54, 59, 67
fragment 98, 54
fragment 99, 72
fragment 101, 54
fragment 103, 70
fragments 105a and c, 70–1, 137
fragment 107, 71
fragment 110a, 69
fragment 111, 69
fragment 112, 69
fragment 114, 70
fragment 115, 69
fragment 120, 71, 73
fragment 121, 149
fragment 125, 149
fragment 126, 63
fragment 130, 126
fragment 131, 71
fragment 132, 54
fragment 140, 67
fragment 141, 69
fragment 146, 71
fragment 147, 139
fragment 155, 72
fragment 168b, 71
Sardis, 53, 54–6, 84, 144
schoolmistress, Sappho as, 123
Scudéry, Madeleine de, 121
sexuality, history of, 127
Shakespeare, William, 140
Sicily, 35, 43, 53, 80, 108, 122, 137–8
Sidney, Sir Philip, 87, 140
Simonides, 98–9
slavery/slaves, 29, 38, 48, 54, 83–4, 87, 91, 92, 101, 102, 106, 137–8, 150, 151–2, 165–6, 169
Socrates, 50, 91–2, 94–7, 162
sodomy, 166–7
Solon, 97, 160
song, 39, 54, 64, 68–70, 130, 155
Sophokles, 11, 114, 129, 133
Sparta, 14
stanza, Sapphic, 16, 105
Stesikhoros (Stesichorus), 35, 43, 47

Stoicism, 169
Stonewall, 158
Suda, 35, 68, 82, 87
suicide, 88, 109, 124, 126–7, 133
Swinburne, Algernon Charles, 125–6

Telesilla, 27, 86, 161
Tennyson, Alfred, Lord, 142
Terence, 102
Thanatos, 10
Tithonos, 21, 147–8
tragedy, 90, 100, 104, 114
tragic heterosexual, Sappho as, 110
transgender, 118, 125
translation, 139–53
transvestism, 118, 124, 125, 126, 139, 140
tribadism, 119, 161
Troy, 13, 14, 19, 20, 21, 29, 36–9, 42, 75
Tullius Laurea, 101
tyrants, 77–8
Tzetzes, Johannes, 111

vases, 27, 69, 93–4
 Sappho on, 93–4
Verlaine, Paul, 123
Virgil, 87, 104–6, 140, 160
Vivien, Renée, 123

war, 14, 15, 19, 31, 37, 44–5, 66, 78, 90, 144, 159, 165–6
weaving, 14–15
wedding, 38–40, 47, 57, 68–70, 71, 104
West, M. L., 143
Wharton, Henry Thornton, 125, 128
white rock, 88–90, 109, 126–7, 133, 141–2
Williams, William Carlos, 143
wine, 39, 66, 69–70, 106, 132
Winkler, John J., 163–4
Wittig, Monique, 124, 155–7

Yourcenar, Marguerite, 124

Zeus, 34, 51, 57, 75–6, 89, 147, 151–2